STEPS TO ACHIEVEMENT
FOR THE SLOW LEARNER

MARYLOU EBERSOLE, M.S.Ed.

Principal and Guidance Director,
Warren Achievement School

NEWELL C. KEPHART, Ph.D.

Executive Director, Achievement Center
for Children, Purdue University

JAMES B. EBERSOLE, M.D.

Chairman of Board of Directors,
Warren Achievement School

STEPS TO ACHIEVEMENT FOR THE SLOW LEARNER

CHARLES E. MERRILL PUBLISHING COMPANY

Columbus, Ohio   *A Bell & Howell Company*

125

THE SLOW LEARNER SERIES
edited by Newell C. Kephart, Ph.D.

©1968 by Charles E. Merrill Publishing Company, Columbus, Ohio. All rights reserved. No part of this book may be reproduced in any form, by mimeograph or any other means, without permission in writing from the publisher.

Library of Congress Catalog Card Number: 68-14967

ISBN 0-675-09668-5

4 5 6 7 8 9 10—72 71

Printed in the United States of America

to

PROFESSOR ROBERT K. ENDERS

in appreciation of his
contributions through teaching

Preface

It is hoped that this text will contribute to the understanding and teaching of the slow learner. In most respects, the information and material submitted here apply to children with learning disabilities, regardless of the cause of the disability or the chronological age of the child. This guide is recommended for teachers, therapists, physicians, students, and parents. The learning theory presented in the first half demonstrates the importance of careful medical, educational, and psychological studies of the child to insure maximum readiness for learning. In addition, the theory stresses purposeful teaching methods to help the child perceive the information in his environment accurately and efficiently.

The curriculum in the second half of the text is divided into systematic learning steps necessary for positive, educational goals. It is well recognized that visual, auditory, and tactual techniques are appropriate for teaching the slow learner, but it is necessary to organize these into well-defined subject areas so that the teacher is aware of what to teach for a definite destination. Motor activities, the importance of which are presented in "The Slow Learner in the Classroom" (Kephart, 1960), are effectively used as basic steps to achievement in a carefully planned, school program of pre-academic and then academic studies. This curriculum guide is not to be used as a cookbook. The steps must be adapted to the child's individual needs and abilities. The teacher is challenged to add additional methods for the reinforcement of each learning step.

The completion of this book was dependent upon the counseling and assistance of many persons and organizations who are aware of their contributions, although it is impractical to identify each.

At the Warren Achievement School for Handicapped Children in Monmouth, Illinois, the dedication of the staff to the task at hand has been most commendable and heart-warming. Much of the material presented here has been developed and put to the test in this facility, a diagnostic and teaching center supported by the Mental Health Department of Illinois and the citizens of Warren County.

Capable assistance and support have been available from the staff of the Achievement Center for Children at Purdue University in Lafayette, Indiana.

Our understanding of the medical and family counseling needs of the handicapped child rests to a large degree on the personal dedication of Dr. Robert E. Bruner of the Cerebral Palsy Center, Kansas City, Missouri.

The art work presented in this book was developed through the interest and talent of Mrs. Charles Mercier, Wilmette, Illinois.

A grant from the Sears-Roebuck Foundation has provided financial assistance for preparation of the manuscript.

To these, and many others, we express sincere appreciation. The plight of the slow learner is being somewhat understood and alleviated through their selfless efforts.

MARYLOU EBERSOLE
NEWELL C. KEPHART
JAMES B. EBERSOLE

1968

Contents

125

Chapter 6   65

The Developmental Stages of Learning

Chapter 7   75

Conceptualization

Chapter 8   97

Arm and Hand Coordination

Chapter 9   109

Cutting with Scissors

Chapter 10   121

Pre-Reading

Chapter 11 145

Pre-Writing

Chapter 12 165

Pre-Arithmetic—Counting and Number Concepts

Appendix 183

Index 193

chapter 1

Special Needs of the Child
Handicapped by Brain Damage

Who is a handicapped child? He is a human being who deviates from capabilities we expect from any normal child. He may deviate a little, or a lot; he may have only a single learning disability, or combinations of learning disabilities. Many handicapped children are similar, but no two are exactly alike. The children will vary in their needs for three definite reasons: 1. All children are born with innate, inherited characteristics; 2. Each child responds to his particular environment; 3. The *number of areas*, the *place*, and the *degree* of brain damage will never be the same in any two cases.

Possible areas of brain damage in three different children may be represented diagrammatically by dark spots in the brain region. (See Fig. 1-1, p. 2.)

The child's progress depends on the genuine, continued cooperation of his parents, educators, and physicians; and on an accurate understanding of his *individual* needs.

EVALUATING FOR A SPECIALIZED CURRICULUM

There has been a tendency to categorize brain-damaged children and, at least by implication, to assume that the resulting group is homogeneous in respect to learning needs. However, educators are be-

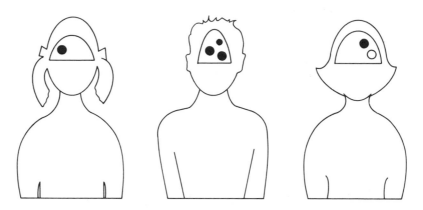

FIGURE 1-1. No two children with brain damage are exactly alike: the area and degree of damage vary.

ginning to evaluate each child as a distinct individual who can benefit from an educational program planned especially for him.

Some children with brain damage have neurologic abnormalities, such as paralysis, reflex changes, abnormal motor patterns, abnormal EEG changes, and convulsions, which make diagnosis of the problem relatively easy by the age of two years, or even earlier.

There are, however, a sizable number of children who have what is termed *minimal brain dysfunction syndrome* which is less easily diagnosed. These children often have relatively minor abnormalities at an early age, including irritability, hyperactivity, short attention span, mild clumsiness, and emotional lability. They are considered by the parents and doctor to be just "irritable babies" and are expected to "grow out of it." However, the first few years in school bring evidence of specific learning deficits such as reading slowness, poor spelling, and difficulty with abstractions and whole-part relationships.

Because of a lack of demonstrable neurologic abnormalities, many of the children with minimal brain dysfunction are diagnosed as behavioral or emotional problems. Actually, these children are showing the frustrations of repeated failures. Until their problems are recognized as those of true brain damage, with attendant limitations of performance in certain areas, their problems will be aggravated by the demands and expectations of our scholastically oriented society.

Specific educational programs should be based on evaluations of *how* the brain damage has affected the child's abilities to learn. Psychological and medical evaluations should include diagnostic data related to the efficiency of the child's perceptual senses, the ability of the child to correlate thoughts, and the effectiveness of the child's muscles and neurons to respond in a meaningful way.

A teacher may be confronted with the inaccurate coloring pictured in Fig. 1-2. Diagnostic tools can pinpoint the reasons causing the child to color in this way. The remedy is not "more practice in coloring," but rather a carefully planned curriculum to correct the underlying inabilities. The child may be unable to see well; he may be unable to control his hand or fingers; he may be unable to correlate what he sees with his manual performance.

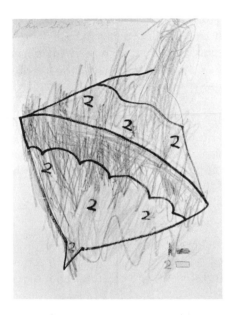

FIGURE 1-2. It is important to *diagnose* carefully why an 8-year-old brain-damaged child colors this way.

There is a direct relationship between *when* and *how* the handicapped child begins his remedial work and how successful he becomes in his learning. The majority of children with special learning needs do *not* "outgrow" their handicaps, and they cannot take advantage of an education without extra assistance. When a learning problem is first suspected, remedial learning activities should be initiated immediately. Because of the child's inability either to find or to interpret stimuli in his environment, we must bring discoveries and correlations to him in a *deliberate* manner.

Handicapped children benefit most from an education during the

"Golden Years": approximately three to ten years of age. If the brain-injured child is not effectively educated, his IQ may drop as much as two points each year. As a child becomes older, he builds up defenses and habits which are difficult to break through before learning can begin. The child's motivation is hindered by responses conditioned by too many failures.

There are no infallible teaching methods. Often, there can be no absolute medical diagnosis for the brain-damaged child. Therefore, a teacher cannot rely entirely on a diagnosis or a standard curriculum, but is challenged to find appropriate methods according to the individual needs and responses of the brain-damaged student.

The curriculum for handicapped children does *not* evolve by simply *reducing* the curriculum content used for normal children, or by emphasizing *more drill* on the same methods used to teach normal children. Handicapped children need to be taught:

1. *With methods specifically adapted to individual needs.* Emphasize a teaching approach through the sensory avenue by which the child learns best, yet also strive to improve learning by way of sensory approaches which, in the past, have not been too effective for him.

2. *With an emphasis on concrete techniques,* even when abstract subjects are being taught. (See Chap. 7.)

3. *With a curriculum that builds upon itself,* so that objectives are accomplished by way of a well-planned series of learning steps. Evaluate carefully to be sure the child is ready for each successive step.

4. *With the understanding that there are three teaching levels:*
   a. a TOLERANCE level at which it is easy for the child to work;
   b. a level at which it is a CHALLENGE for the child to apply himself;
   c. a level at which it is FRUSTRATING for the child to try.
   Present teaching materials applicable to either of the first two levels, depending upon the objective of the lessons and the child's ability to cope with studies that day.

5. *With a variety of methods that reinforce one another.* (See Chap. 4.)

6. *With curriculum objectives that encourage generalization.* Generalization is the application of specific skills to many purpose-

ful activities. (For example, crawling, walking, hopping, and skipping are used for the purpose of locomotion.) Generalization permits a broad basis for conceptualization and allows for variation and adaptation. Particularly with the minimally damaged child, much of our difficulty in teaching may be the result of not laying an adequate foundation on which the child can begin to build generalizations.

7. *With a varied and interrelated curriculum that:*
    a. *rotates active and passive activities* to prevent boredom and fatigue;
    b. *relates activities* so that one "flows" into the next, avoiding drastic "changing of gears" which is so difficult for brain-damaged children;
    c. *varies the length of the lessons* according to the attention span of the child or children.

TEACHING HOW TO STUDY

Listen carefully to what the child says. His comments are valuable clues to his responses, and he will express many feelings that will give you deeper insight into his needs.

Brain-damaged children do not learn as automatically as do normal children. Therefore, "teaching *how to learn*" becomes as important as the systematic presentation of new materials to be learned. If a child cannot effectively learn *how to use* educational stimuli presented to him, both the child and the teacher waste valuable time with lessons that are not meaningful.

In the normal classroom, it has always been accepted that the best students are those capable of independent projects, since they are responsible and have a natural curiosity. Incongruous as it seems, brain-damaged children also must learn to work independently. In a classroom where the child's need is unique, it is impossible to have enough staff to meet each need. Many self-help methods must be employed so that the children may learn to help themselves and each other.

Since attention is a selected response, it is usually more difficult to achieve motivation (the "kicker") in a brain-damaged child than in a normal child. The response of the child can be manipulated by the teacher or parent, as demonstrated by one mother in clearing her home of a large group of noisy neighborhood children. She announced, "When you get ready to go home, I have some cookies for you." "Bribes" or "rewards" may aid motivation. The "M and M Method" (candy as a reward) and cards with pretty stickers are well recognized. Eventually, however, motivation for learning should come from desires *within* the child because he derives satisfaction from what he accomplishes.

While motivation is dependent upon the responses achieved by the child, it is also dependent upon the stimuli presented to him. Teaching materials, such as dittoed or mimeographed sheets, may be used for teaching brain-damaged students. But *why* and *how* to use them are important considerations:

1. *Is the ink dark enough? Is the printing clear?*
   Dittoed lessons are notorious for being blurred or faded. Visual shortcomings are closely associated with some brain damage. The teaching problem may be compounded by the lack of definite contrast between the symbols and the paper.

2. *Is spacing adequate?*
   Consider the spacing between letters and words. Where visual problems are prominent, letters tend to run together; they may even appear to move about. Therefore, allow adequate and definite spacing between the symbols. If necessary, cut the words or syllables apart and remount them farther apart on another paper (even a colored paper). Consider spacing between lines, so that the lines are not so close together as to become visually jumbled. Draw a prominent horizontal line between rows of printed words, or cut the rows apart, so that the student works on one row at a time. An arithmetic lesson (to fill in the missing numbers) printed as:

   1,   ,   3,   4,   ,   6,   ,   8,   ,   10

   may have to be revised, for example:

Note that the symbols are substantially larger and farther apart, numerals are boxed or underlined, and fewer numbers appear on the line.

3. *Do the lessons progress too rapidly?*
   Normal children can learn at a more rapid pace than brain-damaged children. When a dittoed lesson presents a progression of numbers to manipulate, prepare the special-education material so that it moves slowly and allows opportunity for relearning and reinforcement of learning.

PROJECTING THE CURRICULUM

When a child enters his first public school program, he is assumed to have already mastered basic readiness skills which will qualify him to begin a mastery of the symbolic materials. Visually, he will be presented with words, diagrams, and similar representations on a printed page. Verbally, he will be expected to manipulate conceptual items and to deal in intricate, logical sequences.

The fundamental assumption that most children have progressed adequately to begin school studies at the age of five or six, or even earlier, is correct. However, in a significant percentage of children, including the brain damaged, accidents occur during the developmental period which interfere with the establishment of a stable perceptual-motor world. Concepts of space and time may be distorted. There may be varying degrees of motor deficits. As a result, many children come into school systems lacking basic readiness for much of the material to be presented.

Before the brain-damaged child enters a normal kindergarten program, three phases of educational processes are needed, as diagrammed in Fig. 1-3, p. 8.

It is recognized that no curriculum can be clear-cut. Learning areas overlap. Socialization, discipline, and correction of motor deficits will be elements of learning at all phases. And, in all phases, well-established norms of the development of children should be considered.[1]

ACCEPTING—A PRELUDE TO LEARNING

Three interrelated types of acceptance concern the child: 1. The child's acceptance of himself; 2. The child's acceptance of others; 3. The acceptance of the child by others. The consideration of these is imperative before a child can respond well to formal education.

THE CHILD'S ACCEPTANCE OF HIMSELF

Any child needs to be wanted, loved, respected, and identified for his own capabilities. The handicapped child is beset with fears and

[1]Arnold Gesell, *The First Five Years of Life* (New York: Harper & Row, Publishers, 1940), and Arnold Gesell and Frances L. Ilg, *The Child From Five To Ten* (New York: Harper & Row, Publishers, 1946).

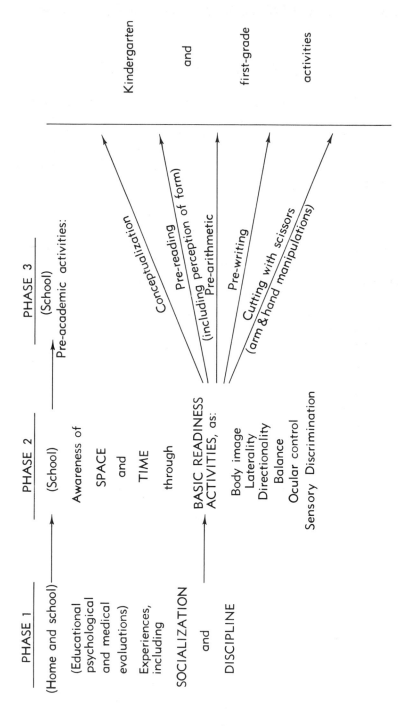

FIGURE 1-3. Three educational phases should precede the kindergarten or first-grade schooling of the brain-damaged child. (Refer to p. 7.)

frustrations about his own shortcomings. He has "felt" the disappointment of those about him, and he requires extra encouragement and reassurance in terms of what he can accomplish. While love must neither smother nor overprotect him, he must feel the security it gives.

It is very important that some explanation be made to the child concerning his handicap. Neurological details are, of course, beyond his comprehension. Weigh carefully what is said in the child's presence. It is not necessary that he share all the apprehensions that may be expressed in visits to a physician or in counseling sessions. Anxiety is contagious. But parents can explain that at one time the child was very sick, and that now he is getting better. A parent might continue, "You are not attending school with some of the other children because you need special help. So we will all work together to help you." A positive approach should always be maintained. Then the child will not think that he is being excluded because he is a "bad child" or because "no one likes him" or because "he can't do anything."

It is interesting to watch the response of a positive, frank approach in the classroom. The child knows he needs help, his friends know he needs help, and the teacher knows he needs help. A teacher may observe, "Joey, it is hard for you to hold a pencil, isn't it?" Joey will readily admit this—and often his eyes will show relief because at last he has found someone who knows he has this trouble! The teacher can continue, "Let's try to help that. Come to the chalkboard, and practice with the chalk. We will also do some hand exercises. Soon it may be easier for you to hold the pencil." There is yet a child to be found who does not respond willingly to such an honest approach. His learning will be motivated by the goal you have established together. Rapport will exist because he knows you are honest. A friendship will be started because he knows you care about helping.

To parents, the child is always a child; to teachers, the child is a student; but it is in leaving home and being with other people that the child tests his right to be an individual and discovers *who* he really is. The first searching for identity (at a mental age of five or six) is tempered by the formal disciplines of the classroom and the informal disciplines of group interaction. Inevitably, there is a conflict within the child as he struggles for autonomy against the forces of well-meaning parents and teachers, whom he cannot do without because of his physical or mental limitations.

Answers to "Who Am I?" and even "Who are you?" can be provided by skillful teaching and guidance. Teachers and parents should not confuse a child's desire for independence with a lack of respect. If normal autonomy is not encouraged, the frustrated and hostile child may become preoccupied, extra-curious, or aggressive. One child overcompensated by eating only what he prepared for himself. Grotesque sandwiches and a messy kitchen resulted from his search for independence, but soon his eating conformed again to the family routine.

There is no magical moment at which the child is ready to hold his own in society. Getting along in the world is a *gradual* learning, maturing process which starts at an early age as a child explores his actions and reactions and those of others. The handicapped child who has been allowed to experience normal, everyday living eventually adjusts to jobs more quickly than the child who is overprotected.

THE CHILD'S ACCEPTANCE OF OTHERS

If a child has accepted himself, he can begin to accept others. At first, he may seem "out of contact" and his responses to others may be masked by many undesirable behavioral characteristics, such as perseveration, distractibility, and disorganization. (See Chap. 2.) The teacher is challenged to find ways to evoke meaningful responses and participation. Clues that disclose a child's acceptance of others include: sharing toys, imitating others, laughing at what someone else does, touching someone, giving "gifts" to please others, listening to others speak and then responding by actions or words, playing games with others, reacting to suggestions without hostility, accepting "gifts" from others, helping classmates, and identifying with friends.

ACCEPTANCE OF THE CHILD BY OTHERS

As the handicapped child becomes aware of his differences, it remains for him to take advantage of his good qualities. The attitude and help of others can mean the difference between his success or failure.

> Authorities agree that the actual handicap is of less importance than the attitude that the family holds toward the child.[2]

The child must experience the "giving" as well as the "taking" of trust. Responsibilities, such as the opportunity to do family chores and to earn money, will indicate to the child that he is trusted. At the same time, adults can respond with appreciation to the child's trust in them.

---

[2]John Charles Wynn, *How Christian Parents Face Family Problems* (Philadelphia: The Westminster Press, 1955), p. 134.

School tasks may include: errands, picking up, putting away, erasing the chalkboard, getting milk, passing papers, and passing the waste-basket.

FAMILY ADJUSTMENT

Parents of a handicapped child require extra consideration, as the initial shock of learning that their child is brain damaged is not easily, if ever, overcome. The family's adjustment may take months or years; and divorce rates are high among couples with handicapped children. The severity of the handicap does not determine how well parents handle the problem.

The needs of the handicapped child should not detract from those of his normal brothers and sisters. Psychiatrists emphasize that other children in the family should understand the handicapped child's problems, and feel free to discuss them. They can then intelligently explain the problem of their brother (or sister) to their friends and school-mates. Normal children must be reassured that the handicap is not "contagious"—that they will not wake up with the same thing some morning!

While much of the burden lies with the mother, the responsibility is felt by the whole family. It is important that family members "share" their concerns so that "repacing" of family activities can be for the advantage of all. The mother should have time each week to escape, and to enjoy a special interest of her own.

All educational, psychological, and medical consultants are not yet in agreement about the rearing of a brain-damaged child. Consequently, the parents find themselves "in the middle," making decisions as they listen to varying advice. Religion and love may aid family adjustment as *supporting* agents. Special-education programs include opportunities for the parents, as well as for the child, to learn. Some programs have increased parents' understanding by teaching them how to work with other handicapped children, as well as with their own. Opportunities for parents to "share" experiences are extremely valuable. At one conference, a mother expressed, "I cannot understand my parents. They expect Billy to be *extra*-good because he is handicapped, and it is too much pressure for all of us." Another mother replied, "But you are fortunate. Because my child is handicapped, his grandparents never expect anything from him."

Parents should not excuse the child's unawareness of such aspects of life as birth, death, sex, and disappointments. These should be explained to handicapped children, even though the explanations may have to be simple and repetitious.

The dental care of handicapped patients has often been sadly neglected. Children with multiple congenital defects may also have dentofacial deformities. Oral clefts (lip or palate) are the most common, and are usually surgically correctible. Other problems (such as malocclusions) unassociated with the child's primary brain damage are present in the same proportion as with the normal child population.

Disturbances in the formation and calcification of teeth are common in handicapped children. Brain damage or illness prior to birth or in the first few years of life may affect the teeth at a critical stage of development, causing missing teeth, or teeth markedly malformed. Poor enamel formation creates not only unsightly cosmetic problems, but also allows the early formation of cavities and rapid "wearing-away" of affected teeth.

Although dental problems may be insignificant compared to the child's muscular or intellectual defects, dental hygiene, both as practiced at home and in the routine care by the dentist, is important. Adequate, timely brushing more than makes up for the psychic energy expended by the mother at a later date in attempting to care for a neglected mouth.

The dentist's understanding of a child who has motor incoordination or emotional problems is necessary to give adequate office dental care. Sedation or even anesthesia are frequently used and are most helpful.

Encouragement to eat proper types of foods is very important. Not only is a well-balanced diet necessary, but the eating of pulpy (detergent) foods acts as an effective cleansing measure; supplementing that which is done with the toothbrush at home. Apples, oranges, sugar-free chewing gum, and other pulpy types of foods should be encouraged, rather than sweets or soft foods. It is surprising how many handicapped children exist on mushy, sweet foods because of difficulty in chewing and swallowing. This insures the creation of major dental problems.

COMPARING THE CULTURALLY DEPRIVED
AND THE BRAIN-DAMAGED CHILD

In many school programs, the culturally deprived child[3] and the child with brain dysfunction are taught in the same classroom. A cul-

---

[3]Note: The culturally deprived child is here defined as one living in a low socio-economic environment. But it is recognized that the brain-damaged child may be "culturally deprived" even in a college professor's family, where the intellectual environment might be so "unobtainable" that he could not begin to try to be a part of it.

turally deprived child, suffering only from retardation due to lack of stimulation (books, creative projects, and conversations), and a general run-down body condition, will benefit by being put into a class with brain-damaged children, where the teaching proceeds at a slow pace, with emphasis in areas of need. However, a culturally deprived child will also benefit just as much by being taught at a very early age (preschool) in a classroom where the curriculum and experiences are simply more *enriched* than in a regular classroom. The teacher of culturally deprived children does not always need specialized training. The progress of a culturally deprived child is usually *predictable*. He may start slowly, but if the teaching is enriched, he will soon get off to a good start, proceeding, without extra help, as a normal child.

In contrast, a brain-damaged child will not profit enough from a curriculum planned only for the culturally deprived child. Educational planning for the brain-damaged includes medical, psychological, and educational evaluations combined to help in localizing the child's areas of *strong* and *weak* learning abilities. The educational program is then two-fold; based on the simultaneous use and refinement of strengths, and the upgrading of weaknesses. For example, a child with eye difficulties can be aided in reading by a more-concentrated-than-normal approach through his sense of hearing. Earphones and a recorder may be needed. The auditory stimulus may need reinforcement by the tactual. Such planning and teaching require a specialized staff, with a teacher particularly trained to instruct the brain-damaged child.

The progress of the brain-damaged child is *not predictable*. As one educator expressed: "I can see a brain-damaged child walk in that door and I can say to myself, 'This child is going to progress rapidly and well.' But two years later I may be disappointed in his abilities. On the other hand, I can see a wreck of a child come in that door and say to myself, 'This child is in such bad shape, I wonder if he'll ever be better.' And a year or so later I am surprised and impressed by the progress the child has made." We can only make a calculated guess as to how a particular child's brain damage is going to influence his long-term learning.

chapter 2

Characteristics and Discipline of the Brain-Damaged Child

The development of the child with brain damage is spotty, with certain childhood characteristics *persisting longer* and being of *greater intensity* than normal. The child may act appropriately for his *mental age*, which is inappropriately low for his *chronological age*. Some tasks requiring well-developed skill may be performed with ease, whereas other, more simple tasks may be particularly difficult.

BEHAVIORAL CHARACTERISTICS

In some cases the brain-damaged child does not exhibit any of the following characteristics, but usually he will have one or a combination of these behavioral responses:

SHORT ATTENTION SPAN—DISTRACTIBILITY—HYPERACTIVITY

Many brain-damaged babies are lethargic, yet irritable for no apparent cause. As the child grows older, he is easily distracted by external stimuli; one stimulus is as vivid and as important as another. The hyperactive child can be compared to an egg-beater that whips a peaceful group into chaos. The noise-level rises when the "egg-beater" arrives, continually moving around, handling persons and objects.

The child's ocular perception, as well as distractions from auditory or tactual stimuli in the environment, need to be evaluated when a child is easily distracted. One little girl kept watching others in her classroom as she tried to do a page of written work. Finally, when the teacher held her head so that her eyes could remain on the work, the child finished several problems. Hoping that the child now recognized what she could accomplish when she watched her work, the teacher released her head. The child tried to work several more problems, sighed in disgust, and begged, "Please hold my head again."

Neurological damage hinders accurate reception and processing of perceptual information. The child may want to do a task, such as tracing a line between two points, but he forgets the task before it is completed, and is unable to perform it as he wishes. Forgetting and lack of accomplishment are tiring and agitating. There appears to be little or no connection between *what* the child observes and *how* he purposefully responds.

The inability of many brain-damaged children to structure and to control their own attitudes and temperaments causes them to react *directly* to the attitudes and personalities of the persons about them. They then *reflect* what they sense or perceive. The atmospheres of the schoolroom and home must be calm and well planned to set an example for patterns of behavior. Ways to lessen hyperactivity include:

1. *Redirect* the child: "Go back and do this." Redirecting will usually elicit a more favorable reaction from the child than will simply stopping an activity. In some cases, it may be necessary first to stop and then to redirect.

2. *Limit work periods* so that the child can achieve success before he gets too tired. (See p. 5, Chap. 1.)

3. *Use some physical contact* with the child, which may be a hand on his shoulder, or a directing of his arm and hand movements.

4. *Avoid teaching at a frustration level.* (See p. 4, Chap. 1.)

5. Help the child to *structure his task* so that he can proceed in a step-by-step manner.

6. *Counsel the child*, helping him to gain insight into his hyperactivity. Handicapped children feel out of place; they know life is falling apart for them and they do not understand that they have a bigger task than do other children whose bodies work normally.

7. *Reduce distractions.* If necessary, provide a cubicle in which the child can work, or place a screen around his work area, and explain why the screen is there.[1] Gradually, if he comprehends, he can cooperate by indicating times he feels less distracted and does not need the screen. Cut out distracting stimuli by the use of medically prescribed pinpoint glasses or ear plugs. Pinpoint glasses should be used with discretion so that appropriate visual fields are seen for limited periods of time. Consider covering a child's eyes while he is *listening* to a lesson. Project materials in a darkened room so that the child can see something only if he looks in the right direction.

One mother expressed unhappiness because her brain-damaged child "went to pieces" when she had some children his age at their home for a birthday party. He could not stay still long enough to enjoy the friends, games, and refreshments. In such a case, one must keep in mind that the child often feels like "blowing his top" as he tries to respond to all of the stimuli about him. *One* friend, or even *one adult* friend may be enough for a birthday party. When the child is able to tolerate *several friends* at a time, the party can still be organized so that, by choice, he can leave the group when pressures become too much. Eventually, a child learns to excuse himself from annoying stimuli for varying periods of time.

What is true of a party is also true of the classroom. *Small groups* will be tolerated better than larger groups. The child who has been removed from the group into an isolated space in the classroom to study may find this limitation so helpful that he will request to be allowed to study in his "office." If the child cannot be excused, supply him with his own private projects, such as coloring or playing with some item, so that he has the opportunity to "mentally retreat" from a group.

8. *Consider medications,* prescribed and supervised by physicians, which help the child to be more calm and relaxed. The physician, school, and home can cooperate by sharing their observations of a child on specific drug therapy.

"Hyperactive homes" are often accused of causing a child's hyperactivity. This may be true in some cases, but usually the overactive

---

[1]W. M. Cruickshank, F. A. Bentzen, F. H. Ratzeburg, and M. T. Tannhauser, *A Teaching Method for Brain-Injured and Hyperactive Children* (Syracuse, N.Y.: Syracuse University Press, 1961).

child originally plants the seeds of hyperactivity, and the home becomes overstimulated as a direct reaction to the child. At this point,
the parents must take definite steps to calm the "*cycle* of hyperactivity."

One observation regarding hyperactivity makes all the efforts of
teachers and parents worthwhile:

> . . . the hyperactivity and driveness of the brain-injured child de-
> creases with the increased functioning of higher mental processes
> . . . our optimism is in the belief that in finding methods to re-edu-
> cate and readjust the perceptual and conceptual disturbances of
> brain-injured children we may be able to lessen their behavioral
> disorders.[2]

Thus, maturation probably will be in the child's favor. And, as new
methods help us to better educate and treat the brain-damaged child,
his hyperactivity can be reduced.

CATASTROPHIC REACTIONS

A catastrophic reaction is an energy-driven, instinctive reaction un-
disciplined (not monitored) by neural control. The child is "out of control"; his responses are explosive and overdone. He may weep, laugh
loudly, or throw himself on the floor. The catastrophic reaction is
often, but not always, born of frustration because the child cannot
cope with a situation which may be very joyful or exciting. Unlike
a temper tantrum, the catastrophic response is not instigated purposefully. The situation should be kept within defined limits, but the
child should not be punished for his reaction. With controls, the child
can receive help from an adult to learn to override his unpredictable
reactions.

DISINHIBITION

Disinhibition is the use of an inadequate, impulsive response. Since
the child does not stop to weigh the consequences of his reactions,

---

[2]Strauss and Lehtinen, "Fundamentals and Treatment of Brain-Injured Children," *Psychopathology and Education of the Brain-Injured Child, Vol. 1* (New
York: Grune & Stratton, 1947), p. 86.

or to consider other possibilities, his responses are inflexible, rigid, and stereotyped. Two examples of disinhibition are:

1. the child who *consistently* knocks articles off a table or a counter as he passes by;

2. the boy who watches his older brother whistle at a girl from the car, and who then wholeheartedly throws himself into the fun by shouting undesirable phrases at other friends.

To overcome disinhibition, teach that there is a *selection* of responses which can be *accepted favorably* by others, therefore giving children a *choice* to make before they react. In this way, *discretion* and *judgment* are introduced.

PERSEVERATION

Perseveration is the inability of the child to alter his attention easily because he is unable to restructure his thinking quickly. Do not confuse perseveration with deliberate lack of response. An inability "to shift gears" in a hurry makes it difficult to meet varying, continuing stimuli and to respond well to a change of directions. It is necessary for the adult to help the child "break his train of thought," or "reorganize his thinking." Examples of perseveration include:

1. The student is asked to draw a horizontal line between two vertical lines, and to stop at the second line. Instead, his horizontal line continues on and on.

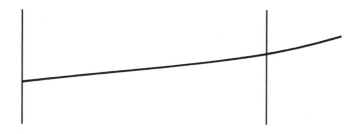

FIGURE 2-1

The teacher should *stop* the child's hand when it reaches the second vertical line, and use also a verbal reinforcement: "STOP."

2. A child seems unable to stop talking, even though he is not making sense. The superficial, continual talking is often referred to as the "Cocktail Syndrome."

3. A child is asked to draw a circle and then a square. He continues drawing circles. *Classroom procedure* can be a mechanism for breaking perseveration. Divert the child's attention to something else, such as a motor activity, before requiring him to return to the drawing of the square.

4. When verbally questioned, the child answers all questions with the same answer he gave to the first.

5. The child has an idea and promotes it despite efforts to divert him. He may fret for hours over a mosquito bite or the loss of some object. This persistence is a type of preoccupation.

One brain-damaged child attended a summer camp and was disturbing the counselors and other children by his negative reactions when given a command to obey. He detained groups by his balking. As the counselors were taught the meaning of "perseveration," they learned that they could warn and remind the child a few minutes early that an event or command was imminent. Then the child had time to "reset" his mind for what was to come. Immediately, he began to follow directions and the undesirable reactions were avoided.

Training exercises may be employed to reduce perseveration. These include:

1. Have the child walk and then stop at a command (verbal, or a whistle, or a sound of any type).

2. Have the child walk and then stop at a designated line.

3. Have the child walk and then stop on a piece of colored paper.

4. Have the child march to music, and stop when the music stops.

5. Have the child walk a designated line, and stop at the *end* of it. The line can be made with chalk on the floor, or with string, colored paper, or even a two-by-four about twelve feet long. (This exercise also reinforces the concept of "beginning" and "end.")

In all of the preceding exercises, the child may start by walking. Then, when he has the idea of the exercise, vary it by running, skipping, hopping, animal walks, etc.

6. Have the child slowly tear a big sheet of newspaper, and *stop* tearing when directed.

7. Have the child continuously pat his hands on a table-top, and *stop* the patting at command.

8. Direct the child to *stop* or to *start* jumping on a trampoline.

9. The *stop light* used in a classroom can reinforce the child's idea of "stop" and "go." START where there is a green color. STOP where there is a red color. To emphasize this concept, use a four-sided box, two sides with a green circle each and two sides with a red circle each. The children respond in various activities to the command from their stop light. By *watching*, the child translates a visual pattern into a motor response. *Telling* the child to go or to stop, translates an auditory stimulus into a motor response.

10. Provide an electrical buzzer system controlled by pressing a button. Direct when to "press the button" and when to "stop." The auditory experience reinforces this technique.

INSTABILITY OF PERFORMANCE

Instability means that something learned at one time may not be retained to use later, forcing the child to live in "a moment of time." He has difficulty remembering things long enough to relate them. One child complained, "I have lost my idea." Ways to help recall include:

1. Be sure the child *completely understands* what he is being taught.

2. *Relate* new situations to those the child already knows well. The old situations act as an anchor to make the new ones more definite.

3. Teach when the child is *well motivated* and ready to work.

4. Use *memory* exercises. (See Chap. 6 regarding visual and auditory memory.)

5. Increase the *intensity* of the task stimulus by:
   a. approaching the task by way of the child's most efficient sense organs;
   b. presenting the lesson in a very vivid manner so that it *stands out* from background activities.

RIGIDITY

An inflexible reaction against a learning situation is called *rigidity* which, if ignored at an early age, may progress so far that no further learning can take place. As continual failures cause a child to resist trying, he decides, "I can't" or "I won't." Distinguish between rigidity, frustration, and actual inability to do a task. *Rigidity* leads to resistance directed at the activity; *frustration* leads to undirected, shattered behavior.

Examples of resistance include having tantrums, getting limp, turning away, shutting the eyes, kicking, biting, ororverbalizing, developing aches and pains, and giggling. When you think you have broken through one resistance, the child invents a new one.

To diagram rigidity, begin with a circle representing the child's actual area of irreversible brain damage. Around that draw a *halo area* of inactivity that develops because the child "backs away" from the first area in which he cannot perform. Although the child *can* function in the halo area, he chooses not to because it is difficult or because he has failed before.

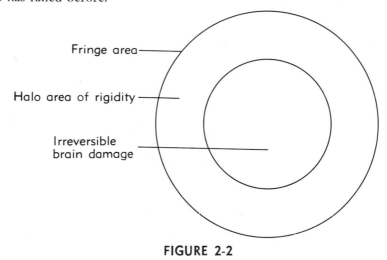

Fringe area

Halo area of rigidity

Irreversible
brain damage

FIGURE 2-2

Approach the problem of rigidity by requiring the child to complete *fringe* activities; i.e., those activities on the border of the halo area which the child still knows he can do. Gradually *push into* the halo area, showing the child that he can achieve. Difficult tasks gradually become easy. "Pushing through" is an organized, continually planned, step-by-step approach as the child works on tasks which challenge but do not frustrate him. Teaching methods for pushing through include:

1. *Keep the work area neat.* Provide *only* the task on which the child is working.

2. *Don't become so emotionally involved with the child* that you worry about him or are not objective about his needs.

3. *Don't take the child's insults personally.* He is usually upset with himself, not you.

4. *Be calm.* Show no anger, irritation, or rejection toward the child.

5. *Speak softly.* Even whisper sometimes, so that the child listens carefully. Never shout.

6. *Be firm.* Do not allow the child to escape a task that you know he is capable of performing. If the child offers resistance, keep working to let him know *he is going to do the job.*

7. *Be consistent.* Don't alternate between giving in to the child and being firm about completing a goal. *Expect* the child to obey.

8. *Use simple commands and directions.* Don't talk too much.

9. *Never ask "Do you want to do this?"* Say, "Do this." The child should not decide if he wants to do what you require. You should structure the task for him.

10. *Be respectful* of the child as an individual in his own right, and when he behaves correctly, tell him that you appreciate it.

11. *Be kind.* But don't gush, overpraise, or overdo your concern, sympathy, and love.

12. *Set up definite work periods,* so that the child can anticipate with security.

As a child grows, the tasks with which he is presented and the activities into which he is thrown become increasingly complex, demanding an integrated, coordinated response of the entire nervous system. The greater the demand for overall response, the more frequent becomes the interference by the child's brain damage, with consequent failure in his response. Rigidity may spread from the initial true halo area of inactivity, causing the child's refusal to attempt virtually any new or different activity. Widespread rigidity, then, comes to interfere with large areas of the child's learning.

Rigidity is related to the complexity of the task, since complexity requires an overall response of the child's neuro-muscular-sensory coordination, not based on the adult's objective judgment regarding the difficulty level of the task. Remedying rigidity involves simplification of the task. A child, however, might well find the coloring of a circle every bit as difficult as the coloring of a rabbit because the neuro-muscular-sensory demands are, in both cases, almost the same. The neuro-muscular-sensory demands of the task may be reduced by providing simpler steps: 1. Pick up the pencil; 2. Color the center of the figure; 3. Color out to the line. The task, thus, is broken down into stages of neuro-muscular-sensory requirements. The child can be pressed to attempt each stage, overcoming his rigidity. As he progresses from stage to stage, the level of neuro-muscular-sensory coordination at which he begins to break down can be observed.

One little girl had difficulty learning to write her name. Reducing the complexity of the task, the teacher attempted to teach individual letters. All went well until the capital "N" was encountered, which engendered a great deal of rigidity and proved to be impossible. In other evaluative procedures it was determined that this child had particular difficulty with diagonal lines. The diagonal stroke of the "N" was the source of her difficulty in learning to write her name. A teacher must be aware not only of the objective coordination requirements of the task, but also of the possible *specific interferences* in a particular child.

VARIABILITY

Just as the brain-damaged child's development is spotty in regard to specific activities, it is also spotty from day to day, or even from hour to hour. Often, brain-damaged children simply do not feel well. They may have a headache, a ringing in their ears, or some inexplicable cause for difficulty in thinking. As one physician expressed to the mother of a handicapped child, "Could you work well if you felt as you do with a fever?"

Distinguish between a child's inability to perform and his unwillingness to perform. The child's variable performance causes people to believe, "This child is not trying today." It is possible that the child is not trying, but it is probable that he needs extra help because it is more difficult than usual for him to perform.

Abortive movements, due to lack of neuro-muscular control, make a child appear unpredictable. An unregulated "pat" will turn into an unintended "poke" or "push."

A brain-damaged child *appears* to be unpredictable because he varies in his basic abilities to *absorb*, to *process*, or to *respond* to different stimuli. He may be good in reading and poor in writing. He may respond well to auditory stimuli and yet barely respond to visual stimuli. A discouraged parent exclaimed, "Sometimes my child does what I want him to do and sometimes he doesn't. Yesterday he did his work very well and today he can't do anything."

Detailed evaluations may actually disclose the child to be very predictable. Strengths, weaknesses, abilities, and disabilities can almost be plotted. Then, it is no longer a mystery how to teach the child more effectively, or how to live more comfortably with him.

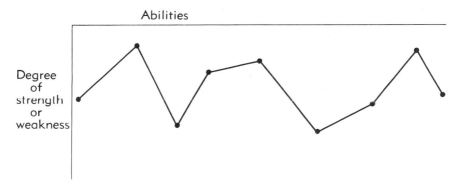

FIGURE 2-3. A diagram of capabilities.

The fluctuations in the preceding graph indicate the inconsistencies typical of many brain-damaged children. The weak areas must be strengthened, since, eventually, there is a correlation between the weak and the strong. If low areas are not improved, the discrepancy between high and low areas becomes greater and the high areas may stop progressing. Therefore, it is necessary to work with both strengths and weaknesses, often stimulating deficient areas *through* strong areas.

DISORGANIZATION

Since the child's neural organization is defective, he is unable to sort perceptual data with which he is confronted. He is unable to *structure* the environment around him into an integrated whole which dictates appropriate behavior. Disorganized responses are the result of this limitation, and are based on only a *part* of the data. They are not signs of deliberate disobedience or wilful wrongdoing. Performance becomes an all-or-nothing attempt, often bizarre and disruptive in nature. The child is mixed up, and dissipates his energies as he tries to do everything at once. He confuses one day with another. He cannot decide what item to put in which drawer, and he has difficulty sorting. He is not sure about the directions he has just heard, or of "when to do what" in new situations.

Perceptual disturbances, however, cause the child to appreciate a structured environment. He likes to know *what* to expect and *when* to expect it; in this way, he is not called upon to reinterpret new data. Thereby, the strain on him is lessened and he is free to attend to specific matters at hand. Some children overcompensate by meticulous organization of their schedules and the objects around them.

The child can be taught to become better organized by providing definite rules by which he can live, with specific times at which to do certain activities. The child learns that when he awakens in the morning there are responsibilities expected of him at home and then at school, as presented in Chap. 7. The general order of classroom activities should be the same each day. Carefully explain new routines and situations. A schedule the child can depend upon and anticipate will aid his organization and lessen his apprehension.

A direction, such as, "Just do what you want to do" may be stimulating for a gifted child, but it holds little meaning for a brain-damaged child, who needs *help with new ideas* and help to carry them out. Brain-damaged children cannot be left victims of their lack of originality or ability to organize. No wonder a child expressed, "Do we *have* to do what we want to do again today?"

DISCIPLINE

CONTROL OR PUNISHMENT?

Discipline, to many teachers and parents, denotes punishment of some sort. However, controlling the child through physical or environmental limitation is a form of discipline especially effective for the brain-damaged child. Through such control, the child can be encouraged or forced through a desired response which otherwise might be interrupted by an unstructured reaction to punishment.

If a normal child is disciplined a few times for a misdeed, he usually learns what is expected of him. But the brain-damaged child may need to be reminded repeatedly. Parents and teachers discover the necessity of PROVIDING CONTROLS for the brain-damaged child *until* he can learn to CONTROL HIMSELF. Control keeps a situation within defined boundaries by limiting the environment of the child so that the number of elements presented to him are ones he is capable of structuring. The control may be *physical*, permitting the child to move through only a specific geographical space. It may be *social*, limiting the number or type of children or adults with whom the child can associate at any one time. It may be *activity oriented*, forbidding certain activities too complex for the child to handle.

Control permits the child only as much stimulation as he can manage and organize. Since his abilities will vary from one activity to another and from one time to another, controls have to be flexible. Limitations will be loose on "good" days and in "good" areas, and they will be tight on "bad" days or in "bad" areas. It is necessary to anticipate the difficulty in organization which the child will experience so that controls can be adjusted to this estimate. At the same time, controls must remain flexible so that, in the event of a "bad guess" or a change in the situation of the child, they can immediately be adjusted to the new situation. In addition to being *flexible*, controls must also be *immediate, consistent*, and *appropriate*. Timing is important to help the child to relate cause and effect. It should be remembered that appropriate controls for one child may not be effective with another.

There should be no punitive aspect to the procedures of control. The child is limited in his participation, not because he has done or will do something bad, but because, only within such limitations can he achieve something good. A limitation of the environment often appears to be in the nature of deprivation. Some people are distressed if, in the event of a party, a handicapped child is not allowed to attend. However, for that child, the only alternative may be distress and confusion resulting from his inability to structure. By limiting his participation, his confusion is reduced and his comfort is increased. He may fuss and rebel at not being allowed to go to the party, but this is a response to the single stimulus: "Can't I engage in an activity which people say is pleasant?" At the party, his response may be entirely different when he discovers that the situation is too complex for him to handle.

The reasons for a child's unique behavior should be understood before using controls. Some of the uses include: breaking perseveration, decreasing distractions, breaking habits, pushing through rigidity, relieving catastrophic reactions, and breaking a task down into its components. Controls include: anticipating moves before a child makes them, putting a child through a directed motor activity, making a child sit still to relax, threatening to punish if certain conditions are not met, substituting one activity for another, distracting a child from an undesirable action, offering a reward for a desired response, and using "signals" (abbreviations).

"Signals," such as alphabetic commands, may be helpful as controls for children who respond well to auditory stimuli. "F—O" can mean: "Take your fingers out of your mouth"; "P—Z—U": "Pull your zipper up"; "B—Q": "Be quiet." A signal is a pleasant "secret" between the parent and child.

Control is a positive approach which, through use, will influence large areas of behavior. *Punishment*, on the other hand, is a negative approach to stamp out certain behavior responses which cannot be tolerated. Punishment may be necessary to teach immediate responses for the safety of the child. The learning resulting from punishment is in the nature of conditioned-reflex learning, affecting only a small part of total behavior.

The amount of disorganization of a specific child will influence the extent to which he can absorb and apply the conditioned learning from punishment. Therefore, what we teach by punishment may be more specific than we have anticipated. A teacher had to deal with a brain-damaged child who had the bad habit of throwing stones at his playmates during the recess period. She systematically punished him whenever he threw a stone, always explaining to him why he was being punished. The child learned his lesson well, and he stopped throwing stones. Instead, he would search about until he found a piece of wood to throw at his classmates.

PROFANITY

This recent newspaper headline is appropriate:

PROFANITY IS BRIEF
ROAD TO FREEDOM

The frustration of a non-achieving child leads him to a disinhibited reaction such as the use of profanity. Also, profanity is something the brain-damaged child can easily use as well as someone else, or even better! It is a satisfying avenue of escape which can amaze and impress a group of friends. A teacher should recognize profanity for the reaction it is, and show disapproval—gradually substituting (by approval) reactions, words, and tasks which will be equally satisfying to the child and yet more constructive to group activity.

TEMPER-TANTRUMS

Temper-tantrums should be distinguished from catastrophic reactions in that the former are *wilful* emotional reactions. Learn to anticipate and stop a tantrum before it starts, sometimes by forcibly holding the child until he relaxes from his state of anger. Tantrums are usually directed at a task to be accomplished. The task should not be removed, but, rather, simplified into steps the child can perform. If control methods are ineffective, punishment may be necessary since the child is deliberately disobeying. A child may throw tantrums for his mother, but not for his father. Children often sense the weak spots of adults, and they play on these weaknesses. Help the child to understand that he is expected to control his emotions.

chapter 3

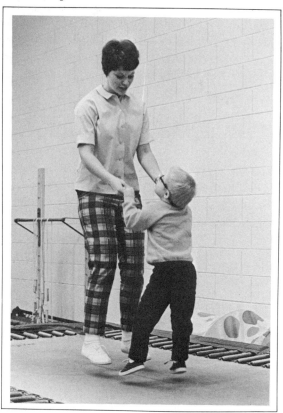

Brain Damage Related to the
Function of the Nervous System

SENSORY, MOTOR, AND INTEGRATING DIVISIONS

The organization of the nervous system can be categorized into three functional divisions:

1. A SENSORY DIVISION
   The *input* or *sensory* function of the nervous system is to receive sensory experiences or stimuli: auditory, visual, tactual, olfactory, and gustatory.

2. A MOTOR DIVISION
   The *output* or *motor* function of the nervous system is to control activities involving smooth and skeletal muscles and the endocrine glands.

3. A PROCESSING AND INTEGRATING DIVISION
   The input and output divisions are related by an intricate *processing* and *integrating* system in the brain that evaluates stimuli so that motor output can be elicited.

Neural pathways connect the three divisions and relay messages from the brain to body parts, and vice versa. A structural (anatomical) or chemical (physiological) change in this system may produce a change in the behavior and learning ability of the individual. A schematic representation of the functioning of the nervous system helps to explain how neural damage affects a child:

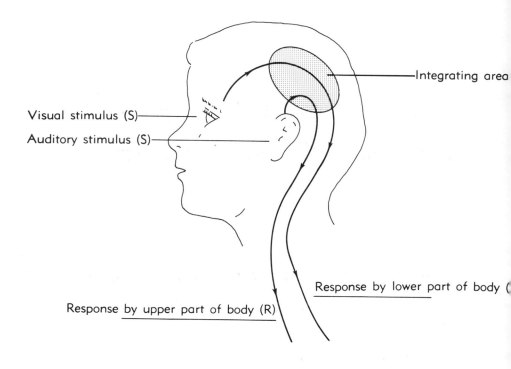

Visual stimulus (S)

Auditory stimulus (S)

Integrating area

Response by lower part of body (

Response by upper part of body (R)

FIGURE 3-1

In this diagram, only two of the sensory input areas are represented: the visual (eye) and auditory (ear). The integrating area is shaded. The response (output) is diagrammed as a response of either the upper or the lower part of the body. The stimulus (S) enters the body by way of a sense organ. It is processed and the child responds (R). Defective sense organs cause the simulus to be limited or distorted. Poorly functioning processing areas cannot integrate information quickly or accurately. Damage between the processing and response divisions may allow the child to perceive and to integrate information, but he may be unable to respond as he should.

TOTAL ACTION OF THE BRAIN

The complex brain, allowing a flexibility of response, is the central controlling area for the nervous system. A response of our body may be the result of the integration of thousands of bits of information. Areas of the brain are now known to be controlling centers for specific body functions including speech, hearing, breathing, vision, and the movement of muscles.

The many parts of the brain cooperate in a functional integration known as *homeostasis*. Homeostasis has been described as a "bedspring effect," since pushing down on one area of a bedspring also begins to pull down surrounding areas. Even uninjured brain parts can be affected negatively by an injury in another area. On the other hand, the homeostasis of the brain may *help to compensate* for an injured area. A neighboring, intact brain area may substitute for, or reinforce, an area that is in trouble. The *homeostasis* and *maturation* processes of the brain indicate why it is not possible to *predict* the progress of a brain-damaged child.

NERVE CELL CHARACTERISTICS
RELATED TO TRAINING

The human brain, the spinal cord, and nerve pathways are made up of billions of nerve cells, or *neurons.*

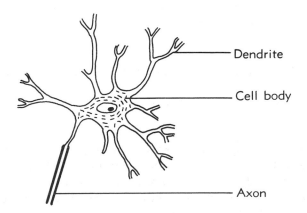

FIGURE 3-2. Diagram of a nerve cell.

The parts of the neuron have specific functions. *Dendrites* are input pathways along which impulses move *to* the cell body. The *axon* is a long, fibrous output pathway that conducts impulses away from the cell body. A neuron has only one axon, but may have more than one dendrite.

Some nerve cells (efferent neurons) conduct messages, or *impulses*, to all parts of the body from the brain. Other nerve cells (afferent neurons) conduct impulses to the brain from the rest of the body. The conduction of neural impulses (neural transmission) through nerve cells is (1) *electrochemical*, and (2) *multi-directional*, involving (3) an *all-or-nothing* response of the nerve cell.

THE ELECTROCHEMICAL IMPLICATIONS OF NEURAL TRANSMISSION

There is no direct contact between one nerve cell and another. Impulses must travel across intercellular space to get from one nerve cell to the next. The impulse travels along a dendrite, across the cell body, and along an axon. At the termination of the axon, electrochemical action sends the impulse through the intercellular space, making contact with a nearby dendrite of another neuron. The junction of an axon of one cell and the dendrite of another is called a *synapse*.

The *agility* of man's brain may depend upon the chemical reactions in his nervous system. The relationship of the chemical nature of message transmission to the inability of some children to learn is still hypothetical. But the question does arise as to whether medications eventually may supplement or stimulate chemical reactions within the central nervous system so that a child can increase his learning potential.

THE MULTI-DIRECTIONAL RELATIONSHIP OF BRAIN CELLS

The neural arrangement of the brain is multi-directional. At synaptic areas, many axons from other neurons may end and converge on a single dendrite.

In Fig. 3-3, p. 35, input involves the branching axons of cells A and B influencing dendrites of cell C. The *summation of the effects* of cells A and B causes cell C to discharge an impulse which is transmitted along the axon of cell C to the right of the diagram. Therefore, within the nervous system there is a constant shift of neural impulses to input and output effects, involving individual nerve cells.

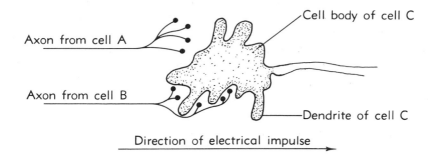

FIGURE 3-3.   Many axons may converge on a single dendrite or nerve cell. (Refer to p. 34.)

Because of their anatomical locations, the terminations of axons are called the *presynaptic* areas, and the ends of the dendrites are called the *postsynaptic* areas.

It is hypothesized that the three-dimensional aspect of neuron arrangement enables a single neuron to be stimulated by axons coming from *many different directions* in the brain. This is important in retraining, as it implies that new brain areas may be stimulated. If the neural impulse cannot reach a particular neuron or develop a reverberating circuit through one route, there may be other directions by way of undamaged neurons through which to reroute the nerve impulses so that learning can take place. This rerouting can be likened to a detour in a highway system. And the training procedures necessary to produce a "detour" of the neural system may often be as difficult and inconvenient as maneuvering most highway detours!

THE ALL-OR-NOTHING ACTION OF A NERVE CELL

A nerve cell reacts to a stimulus by discharging an impulse. A nerve cell *cannot* react with a *partial* response. It reacts with its *total response* or not at all, which is the *all-or-nothing* action of the nerve cell.

Because of this total action, the synaptic stimulus (i.e., the stimulus from axons of other nerve cells) attempting to stimulate a single nerve cell must be strong enough, in summation, to bring about the new reaction. A partial or weak stimulus may not be adequate to cause the next nerve cell to react, but it may have an effect, *facilitation*, on the ability of the postsynaptic neuron to transmit an impulse. Thus, *facilitation* affects the postsynaptic neuron to the degree that it can be excited (caused to act) more easily than usual by stimulation impulses following the first one. Even an inadequate stimulus, therefore, may help the future stimuli to become more effective. *Facilitation* is a conditioning process that sets the stage for a reaction. It can be compared to the heating of water before it boils; the heating helps the water to reach the boiling point. Guyton presents a theory concerning the relationship of *memory* to the storage of sensory information by facilitation:

> Only a small fraction of the important sensory information causes an immediate motor response. The remainder is stored for future control of motor activities and for use in the thinking processes. Most of this storage of information occurs in the cerebral cortex, but not all, for even the basal regions of the brain and perhaps even the spinal cord can store lesser amounts of information.
>
> The storage of information is the process we call *memory*, and this too is a function of the synapses. That is, each time a particular sensory signal passes through a sequence of synapses, the respective synapses become more and more capable of transmitting the same signal the next time, which is called *facilitation*. After the sensory signal has passed through the synapses a large number of times, the synapses become so facilitated that stray signals in the brain can cause transmission of impulses through the same sequence of synapses. This gives the person a feeling of experiencing the original sensation, though in effect it is only a memory of the sensation.[1]

Organized groups of neurons are called *neuronal pools*, which are influenced by stimulations coming to them. Some stimulations cause an immediate reaction; others cause only a facilitation of the combined neural action. It is theorized that a neuronal pool may become a *reverberating circuit*. In this circuit, neurons continually restimulate and influence each other. The result is an *integrated summation* of the total cell grouping. Reverberating circuits could be influenced by different stimuli, but their combined action produces a single response or idea. (See Guyton's theoretical reverberating circuit in Fig. 3-4, p. 37.)[2]

The education of the brain-damaged child takes into consideration two important hypothetical generalizations:

1. POORLY FUNCTIONING AREAS SURROUNDING NEURAL DAMAGE MAY RESPOND TO TRAINING.

---

[1]Arthur C. Guyton, M.D., *Textbook of Medical Physiology*, 3rd ed. (Philadelphia and London: W.B. Saunders Company, 1966), p. 653.

[2]*Ibid.*, p. 673.

A handicapped child may build a "halo area" of psychological inability around a true area of anatomical or physiological inability. Ways to minimize halo areas are given in Chap. 2.

2. UNDAMAGED AREAS OF THE BRAIN MAY SUBSTITUTE FOR DAMAGED ONES. If this substitution does not occur automatically, *retraining* of good brain areas by specific methods of teaching may bring about a desirable substitution or reinforcement. This training is possible if there are not too many neurons destroyed. The basis for this training is *neural facilitation*.

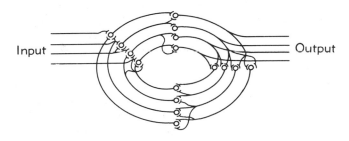

Input   Output

FIGURE 3-4. Guyton's theoretical reverberating circuit. (Refer to p. 36.)

It is important to remember that such compensation is not a simple one-to-one substitution. Because of the intricate interrelationship of parts of the brain and of functions of these parts, any such substitution results in a reorganization of the whole. Consequently, overall functioning is influenced, as well as the specific activity for which a substitute function has been found. It is not enough, therefore, to consider only the substitute activity itself; also to be considered are: (1) the effect upon the whole, and (2) the incidental effects upon other behavior.

DIAGNOSTIC TESTING

The evaluation of a child relies not only on clinical observations but also on other specialized diagnostic procedures. The medical history provides specifics concerning the origin of the child's problem—whether it is familial (with genetic implications); damage to the fetus prior to, at the time of, or immediately subsequent to birth; or some illness or injury occurring during childhood.

An examination by the physician reveals the immediate physical condition of the patient, and allows for observation of his general functions. Congenital malformations, motor activity, sensory function, and behavior should be noted. A gross testing of intelligence can be done, which may require follow-up by psychometric and projective testing performed by qualified psychologists versed in the specific techniques used for children with learning disabilities. A vital part in the evaluation of any neurologic disease is a thorough neurological examination. The examiner must not only be experienced in the procedural complexities, but he must also be aware of influences of developmental changes at various chronological ages of childhood. Some neurological tests require a certain level of mental competence to perform, and even conscious cooperation on the part of the patient.

Consultants, such as for audiometric and ophthalmologic testing, are needed to evaluate specialized functions. Also, a number of highly sophisticated tests are now available for genetic testing (for mongolism) and for the detection of biochemical errors (such as phenylketonuria—PKU). Tests for more complete evaluation of the brain are occasionally needed and include skull X rays, pneumoencephalograms (X rays with air injected in the space around, or in, the brain), angiograms (X rays with radiopaque dye injected into the blood vessels of the brain), or radioisotope scans of the brain. Studies of the cerebrospinal fluid, obtained by spinal tap, may also be helpful. The specialized laboratory procedure most frequently used (in fact, overused) to detect brain damage or dysfunction is the electroencephalogram (EEG).

ELECTROENCEPHAGRAPHY

Nerve cells in the brain produce cyclical electrical voltage. If these cells are damaged, they produce less voltage than do the undamaged cells (similar, perhaps, to the lessened undulations in the tail activity of a tadpole when it is injured). This electrical output can easily be measured by a machine called the electroencephagraph.

It must be remembered that this examination is only one of many tests providing certain information to the physician diagnosing a defect or problem of the brain or central nervous system. It adds valuable information in certain cases, and, in others, it is valueless. Changes in electrical potential, as measured by the EEG, may help localize a brain tumor; or may indicate whether convulsive seizures are due to irritation in specific areas of the brain, to diffuse damage, or to functional disturbances as in epilepsy. However, the disorders shown by the EEG are often disturbances in function only, and no anatomical changes may be seen by the pathologist on gross or microscopic examination of the brain.

Measurable electrical activity appears at about the third month of life. It is of interest to note that the EEG often shows spiking (seizure) activity even when the child does not have clinical seizures. A normal EEG at age six indicates little likelihood of seizure development. Most brain-damaged children who have spikes on the EEG at six years of age, but who have no clinical seizures at that time, will later develop seizures. The clinical evidence of convulsions (seizures) often will appear in an individual up to the age of sixteen years, when the EEG has earlier shown spiking activity.

In taking an EEG, the physician or technician applies electrodes (metal plates with attached wires) to the child's scalp with a special paste. There is no sensation or danger to the child while the tracing is being made. The process is similar to that of an electrocardiogram (EKG), which is a tracing of the heart action. Since it is necessary that part of the test be done with the child asleep, a sedative is frequently administered.

chapter 4

Learning Theory Related to Teaching Techniques

STIMULUS AND RESPONSE RELATED TO INTEGRATION

For years, psychologists believed that there were only two processes concerned with learning theories: (1) the stimulus was presented to an individual and (2) he responded. It was as simple as a single-line telephone system. Soon, it became apparent that different stimuli could produce the *same* response, and that a prediction of response was not always possible. Therefore, learning theory was expanded to include a process of integration *between* the stimulus and response. (See Fig. 4-1, p. 42.)

A *stimulus* is an external agent affecting a person in some way. A *response* is a reaction resulting from a stimulation. *Integration* is neural action within the processing areas of the nervous system, where there is an elaboration of the input resulting from a stimulus.

A response is now recognized to be more complex, influenced by interrelationships, as diagrammed in Fig. 4-2, p. 42.

Input is an internal, neurological activity in response to a stimulus. It directly patterns the stimulus. Output is an internal, neurological response, resulting from integration.

Integration elaborates the first awareness of input. Yet, during and after this integration, the elaborated information is "fed back" to the awareness of the human organism, reaffecting initial attitudes and input. Therefore, the individual's final response to the initial stimulus is

Integration

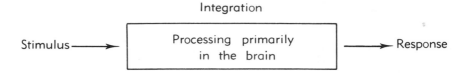

FIGURE 4-1. **Learning includes integration between the stimulus and the response. (Refer to p. 41.)**

tempered by information based on present integration *and* feedback; learning becomes cyclical.

Exactly what happens in the brain during integration is hypothetical. The *Cell Assembly Theory* of Hebb infers that repeated stimulation leads to the development of a *cell assembly*.[1] This assembly is a group of association-area neural cells capable of acting as a closed circuit or of influencing other such neural systems. Assuming that cells A, B, C, and D become associated with one another so that activity in one facilitates activity in the next, the cell assembly is schematically diagrammed as in Fig. 4-3, p. 43. Theoretically, the cell assemblies act as a reverberating circuit (described in Chap. 3) with neural impulses relating one cell to another. A change of response may mean a rearrangement of neural excitations with cells stimulated in a different order. (See Fig. 4-4, p. 43.)

The activity of the closed circuit becomes more *stable* as it is continually stimulated. For a short time it may act as a closed system, even after the stimulation of specific receptor cells has stopped. With learn-

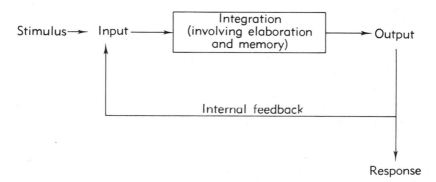

FIGURE 4-2. **A response influenced by interrelationships. (Refer to p. 41.)**

---

[1] D. O. Hebb, *Organization of Behavior* (New York: John Wiley & Sons, Inc., 1949).

ing, the system may become so stable that it no longer needs to depend upon a *continuing* sensory stimulus in order to be effective.

Learning occurs as cell assemblies are stimulated and "fixed." Established assemblies are the basis for future learning, and become a stor-

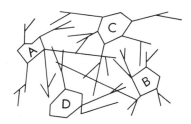

FIGURE 4-3.   A schematic diagram of a theoretical cell assembly. (Refer to p. 42.)

(Refer to p. 42.)

age place for a basic image or idea. Assemblies work together to create more complicated thought processes.

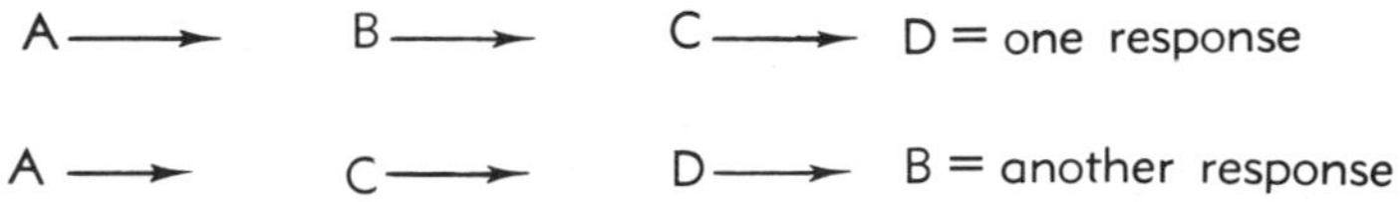

A⟶   B⟶   C⟶ D = one response

A ⟶   C⟶   D⟶ B = another response

FIGURE 4-4

TEACHING TECHNIQUES BASED ON THEORY

Teaching the brain-damaged child is a controlled, *systematic procedure*, guided by a knowledge of the *stimulus-response process* as well as by a knowledge of how the child neurologically interrelates his learning, as presented in the Cell Assembly Theory. Teaching then includes, in order:

1. a comprehensive awareness of the child's abilities, so that the most favorable *avenues of approach* to learning may be employed;

2. *reinforcement and stabilization* of learning, using the *perceptual-motor match* and *distributed practice;*

3. the establishment of meaningful and useful thought processes by *forming and relating cell assemblies.*

AVENUES OF APPROACH

Because of their neurological problems, brain-damaged children must be taught by multi-sensory methods. It is important, however, to organize this multi-sensory approach so that it will add to the child's learning and to the development of his organized information, rather than to his confusion. It is essential that the information presented be related to the child's most adequate source of information as a core.

Thus, when teaching through such multi-sensory methods as those of Fernald, determine *which* sense avenue is most efficient for the particular child.[2] *The principle presentation of information should then be made through this sense with the other sense avenues complimenting it.* Many times a teacher will make the primary presentation through a sense avenue which is a very poor source of information for a certain child. She will then make all other sources, including his strong avenue, auxiliary to this poor source. Since his poor sense gives confused information, the addition of teaching through the other senses only increases the confusion. Thus, a good method of instruction gives poor results.

The method of organizing the multi-sensory presentation will vary from child to child as strengths and weaknesses in the information value of perceptual inputs vary from sense avenue to sense avenue. Thus, the same basic presentation of material will be quite different to one child than it will be to another. It is not so much *what* we present as *how we present it* which makes the difference between success and failure of multi-sensory presentations.

√ Responses are directly dependent upon the accuracy with which stimuli are received and interpreted. The reception, perception, interpretation, and response associated with any sensory stimulation is quite complicated. The best clinical physician may, on occasion, be unable to interpret the problem area accurately. Consequently, in order to avoid any possible omission or misinterpretation prior to the formulation of the child's educational program, it is wise to have complete visual, auditory, and psychological evaluations by specialists familiar with the problems of brain-damaged children.

Even the sensitivity of the skin of the brain-damaged child may be altered by neural damage. For example, a severely brain-damaged child spilled a cup of scalding hot coffee on the front of her legs. For about

---

[2]G. M. Fernald, *Remedial Techniques in Basic School Subjects* (New York: McGraw-Hill Book Co., 1943).

thirty seconds she did not react at all, and, finally, her reaction was very slight. It may be that such children have more widely varying pain thresholds than do normal children. While, as a rule, the sensation of the skin to pain, touch, temperature, etc. may be decreased due to the general reduction in sensory interpretation and response, there are exceptions. A blind child with a normal tactile sensory mechanism often develops this tactile ability, and sometimes also the auditory sense, to a remarkable degree.

When the mother of any normal preschool child is asked if her child hears well, the invariable response is, "I guess so, when he wants to." This implies that the child may "turn on" or "turn off" his auditory mechanism when he so desires. Also, those who do preschool screening tests for hearing find the tests largely unreliable because of the capriciousness of their subjects. When these difficulties of evaluation are applied to the more variable responses of the brain damaged, it becomes apparent that auditory defects are often undetected unless exposed by the most careful testing.

THE PERCEPTUAL-MOTOR MATCH

Visual information is controlled by the direction in which the eyes are pointed (recognizing that visual information is also dependent upon visual acuity and visual fusion). The pointing of the eyes is controlled by extraocular muscles. The child must learn to explore an object with his eyes in the same way in which he previously explored it with his hands. It is important, however, that the exploration with the eyes duplicate the exploration with the hands, so that the resulting information *matches* when it is compared. Two learning tasks arise at this point:

1. The child must learn to manipulate his eyes through the development of patterns of movement in the extraocular muscles.

2. Perhaps more important, the child must learn to manipulate his eyes in terms of the incoming information.

The only way the child can know that his eyes are under control is to evaluate their information. The criterion of ocular control is the *visual information* which results. However, the young child is only now developing a stable visual world with which to evaluate the present perception. Therefore, the body of information which should provide the criterion for ocular control is not yet present. On the other hand, without ocular control the incoming contributions to the body of visual information are inconsistent and spotty. Thus, a continuous dilemma exists: control of the eyes is hampered by lack of a stable visual world, and, at the same time, the stability of the visual world is impaired by lack of ocular control.

The solution to this dilemma is in *motor manipulation*, where the child investigates motorwise and then experiments with the movement of his eyes until they give him information matching his motor information. Since the body of motor information is reasonably stable, he can stabilize the visual information when a match occurs. Through many such experiments, he develops a visual world duplicating his motor world, resulting in a meaningful, related input: the *perceptual-motor match*.

When the perceptual-motor match is adequate, the child can drop out the intervening motor manipulation and use his now stable, more efficient, visual information to control the eyes and his visual input. At this point, all information, either motor or perceptual-sensory input, or motor response, is a part of a stable overall system which gives consistent information wherever it is tapped. Control of both perceptual information and motor response is possible and is part of one consistent system, enabling the child to make his experiences with his environment more meaningful.

It is obvious that such learning will be difficult and will require extensive experimentation. If the learning process breaks down, an adequate match between perceptual information and motor information is not accomplished, and there is limited stability in the perceptual world. The child may not *see* the relationships of right-left, up-down, and so on. The letters on a page do not present a stable directional relationship. Thus, for brain-damaged children the mechanics of the reading task become extremely difficult. To deal with symbolic material, the child requires a stable spatial world. Such a world can be established only through the development of a system of spatial relationships learned first in the *motor* activities of the child and later projected into *perceptual* data. Such a system must be both generalized and extensive.

DRILL VS DISTRIBUTED PRACTICE

Drill is the enforcement of the same, repetitive approach to an exercise over a period of time. If a child drills and drills on a particular learning problem he often gets worse instead of better. The cell assembly theory of neural transmission explains why drill does not have the same learning effect as does *distributed practice;* i.e., a relearning of the same lesson through teaching approaches varying in content and method. During drill, the student is approached by the *same* continued stimulus by way of the *same* neural pathways. New cell assemblies do not have the opportunity to be formed.

With drill, there is always the danger of "splintering." This involves a specific achievement unrelated to the child's general performance, such as the ability to print his own name after months of working to do so under pressure, even when he cannot identify the letters in his name or write any other letters. He is unable to alter this splintered skill or to use it in any other way.

Good teaching of the brain damaged involves approaching material to be learned through a *variety* of techniques, taking advantage of a cell assembly. A teacher should not jump from one approach to another with great haste, but should consider several approaches for *reinforcement* of learning. Good manners, for example, can be taught by reinforcement. (See Fig. 4-5.)

In the illustrated approach to teaching manners, *many sensory ave-*

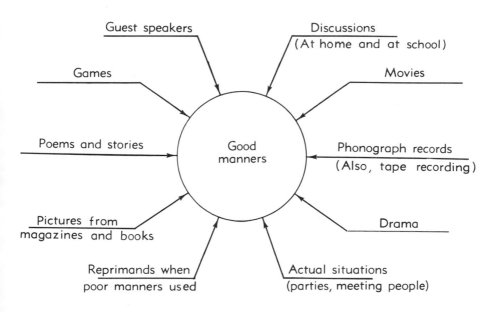

FIGURE 4-5. Subject matter is reinforced by approaching it in varied ways.

nues are employed. Many stimuli are received by the brain to be sorted, elaborated, and integrated in order to stimulate a cell assembly and the resulting purposeful response.

FORMING AND RELATING CELL ASSEMBLIES

An understanding of the theories of *feedback* and the formation of *cell assemblies* gives the teacher a better understanding of WHAT her teaching is to accomplish. An original classroom stimulus may not be enough to achieve the *total* response desired for a child, but it may begin *facilitation* of the neural pattern which in time, with appropriate training, results in desired behavior. Therefore, the child's functioning can be altered by accumulating stimuli.

However, a child is in trouble if any step of the learning process is disturbed, resulting in distortion of the *feedback* information. If the feedback does not *match* or *accurately reinforce* the original input, continued integration leads to confusion rather than to a stabilized input and response.

chapter 5

The Need for a Stable Point of Reference from Which to Interpret Relations

As a child deals with his environment, he deals with spatial and temporal relationships rather than with absolutes. There is no absolute "big"; one object is bigger than another. There is no absolute "before"; one item is before another. Therefore, the child must have a stable point of reference from which to organize his impressions, so that some kind of *order* can be imposed for constructing a coherent totality to the world. His point of reference is his *own body*, which serves as a dependable point of origin of all manipulations.

Through experimentation, a child develops a knowledge of his center of gravity, his body organization, and the position of his body in space. If this experimentation is interrupted, as by perceptual disturbances, poor postural reflexes, or incoordination, the child's knowledge of himself is distorted and unstable. It becomes necessary to *teach* body awareness to the child. The instruction is divided into three categories: (1) Body Image (Body Schema); (2) Laterality and Lateral Midline; (3) Directionality (Spatial Organization).

BODY IMAGE

Body image is a complete awareness of the body and its possibilities of performance, including a knowledge of body parts and their relative positions, as well as an awareness of how much space the body occupies. When brain-damaged children can correctly identify the various body parts, but are only vaguely aware of their relative positions, they lose awareness of a part when its position is altered. Therefore, they react incorrectly when required to move body parts upon command. Body image is discussed at length in *The Slow Learner in the Classroom* in which tests and exercises for establishing body image are recommended.[1] Additional exercises to aid the learning of body image are:

1. Request the child to identify his body parts. *Touch* them so that he can *feel* where they are. Identify the same parts on other persons in the room, and then on pictures of people and animals. Dress and undress a large doll, identifying parts of the doll (also good for hand manipulation).

2. Emphasize the function of body parts: "Where do you taste? Walk? Smell? See?"

3. Using drawing, pasting, or the flannelboard, have the child add missing parts to outlines such as those of a gingerbread man, snowman, jack-o-lantern, and dog.

4. Provide puzzles of people and animals which have changeable body parts.

5. Make puzzles of people, using large catalogue figures or cardboard paper dolls, cutting some vertically and some horizontally. Cut the figure into two parts, then into more parts as the child learns. (See Fig. 5-1, p. 53.)

6. As the child lies against a large sheet of paper, draw around him so that he has a picture of himself on which to put identifying features.

7. Make the child aware that he has two feet by having him jump up and down with his feet alternately together and apart.

8. For short periods of time, put a weight on the arm or leg of the child to make him more conscious of that extremity. This weighting can be accomplished by the use of wrist or ankle bands with lead bars sewn in so that a weight of one-half to one and one-half pounds is provided. The purpose is to make the child conscious of the limb; therefore, alternation is desirable. If the weight is left

---

[1]Newell C. Kephart, *The Slow Learner in the Classroom* (Columbus, Ohio: Charles E. Merrill Books, Inc., 1960).

FIGURE 5-1. Puzzles of people: both horizontal and vertical cuts.

on for long periods of time, adaptation occurs and the cueing effect is reduced. Therefore, apply the weight for only a short period, remove for a period, apply again, and so on. (Be sure,

FIGURE 5-2. A person depicted by gummed crepe paper and crayons.

however, that this technique does not interfere with techniques of the physical therapist.)

9. Make "people pictures" by varying methods. (See Fig. 5-2, p. 53.)

LATERALITY

Laterality is an *internal awareness* of a right and left side. When laterality is established, the child uses right and left sides automatically. How convenient if, to teach the concept of laterality, we could simply draw a vertical line down the middle of a child and explain, "This is your right side and this is your left!" But such simplified teaching is not possible for many brain-damaged children who must experiment until they *feel and realize from their own movements* (kinesthetic feedback) that their bodies are balanced by right and left areas. The child should know not only that a movement *is* on the right side or on the left, but also *how far* to the right or to the left. He must develop a right-left gradient with his movements, in terms of his relationship to gravity.

The awareness of right and left develops and stabilizes from the use of *balance* and *posture*. The child learns that if he leans too far to the right and does not correct himself by leaning to the left or by supporting himself better, he will fall over. It is not uncommon to observe a brain-damaged child who has not had the opportunity to elaborate his movement and postural activities. His movements are rigid and limited. His postural adjustment is so inflexible that he is unable to vary far from a position safely relating to his center of gravity. Therefore, while exercises can be used which specifically emphasize the use of right and left arms and legs, these exercises should never be isolated from the improvement of postural adjustment. *For optimal results, balance exercises should precede and then be included with laterality exercises.*

With the development of an awareness of laterality, a child should also develop a sense of the vertical, since his right and left sides are bisected by an unseen, vertical plane called the "lateral midline."[2] Often, children with brain dysfunction are unable to cross this imaginary midline with any purposeful movement. Thus, an object located to the right of the midline is grasped with the right hand, and any to

---

[2]Jack D. Dunsing and Newell C. Kephart, "Motor Generalizations in Space and Time," in *Learning Disorders, Vol. I,* Jerome Helmuth, ed. (Seattle, Washington: Special Child Publications, 1965), p. 105.

the left, with the left hand. Moving an object from one side to another may even cause a break in an activity, with a shifting of the
object from one hand to the other. A break in continuity of eye
movement may occur in following motion across the child's midline.
Effective activities for overcoming midline problems are discussed
by Kephart.[3] An effective exercise is the placement of ordinary golf
tees into the holes of an acoustical tile. Offer the tee to the child from
varied positions related to his midline. The child should *look* at the
tee, *grasp* it, and then place it, as the teacher directs, into the tile.

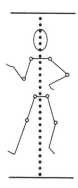

FIGURE 5-3. A lateral midline develops with laterality.

Laterality becomes very important in spatial orientation since it
forms one of the coordinates of the space surrounding the child. Exercises to teach balance and laterality are:

1. Brace a seven-foot, two-by-four board above the floor. (Construct the braces so that they will hold the board when it is
   turned either way.) If children have great difficulty with balance, put the walking board directly on the floor, or provide
   a board six inches wide, or tape or mark a wide line on the
   floor. Have the child move frontwards, backwards, and sideways. Teach him to keep his balance when purposefully handicapped while carrying a heavy or unwieldy object. Have the
   child experience a *shifting* of his body weight by walking
   along with one foot on the walking board which is braced
   above the floor, and the other foot *on* the floor.

---

[3]Kephart, *The Slow Learner in the Classroom*, pp. 170f, 246.

2. Use the *balance board* for *variations* in balance.[4] Provide a very low square (with rounded edges) under the board for beginning exercises. Put strips of non-skid tape on the surface of the board.

3. Hang a punching bag from the ceiling. Instruct the child to hit the bag continually with one hand, and then the other. When he can do this easily, require him to *alternate* his right and left hands as he hits, so that he is forced to *shift* his weight. Punching bag activities can be used as the child stands, or as he kneels. Vary this activity by using a pillow tied in the middle, or a tether ball.

4. Instruct the child to walk *inside* the sections of a ladder on the floor. Then have him balance while walking *on* the rungs and edges of the ladder.

5. Roll a ball to the standing child, directing him to raise his right or left leg so that the ball can roll under it. (To do this well, weight *shifting* is necessary.)

6. Teach the game "Statue," so that children balance in an awkward position.

7. Have the child walk on the ties of a railroad track.

8. Have the child ride a scooter and a bicycle.

9. Have the child practice animal walks.

10. Encourage trampoline activities. These do not need to be precarious, but should incorporate exercises coordinating one body area with another, as: jumping while holding the hands on the top of the head; jumping, bringing up the knees so they can be touched with the hands (intermediate activity); performing "jumping jacks" (advanced activity).

11. Ask the child to raise his right or left hand, or right or left foot. Increase the speed of the verbal directions, as the child learns.

12. Draw a circle on the floor, requesting the child to put his right or left foot into the circle. Use a table-top to do this exercise with the hands. Speed up the activity as the child learns.

13. Sing and act out the "Looby Lou" song with the child.

14. Have the child examine a pair of gloves and ask, "On which hand does each glove go?" Do the same with a pair of shoes.

---

[4]*Ibid.*, pp. 222ff.

15. Have the child push an object across the floor with his knee or elbow.

16. Make colored shapes on a big piece of paper. Instruct, "Put your right hand on the red circle" or "Put your left hand on the green square." (This is also a good exercise for form perception, although instructions may have to be simplified if the child's color or form perceptions are limited.) To simplify the task, put several objects which the child *can identify readily* on the table, asking him to put a specific hand on a particular object. Flat objects are least distracting. Be sure the child has to use each hand on each side of the midline. Vary this technique by asking the child to place the right or left foot at specific places on a floor pattern.

17. Draw right and left hands and feet on the sides of a block. "Roll the dice" and ask the child to identify the side that is up.

18. Hold a single object in front of the child, instructing him to pick it up with a particular hand. Again, be sure the child uses both hands, crossing the midline occasionally. Increase the speed of the directions as the child learns.

19. Have the child move a ball across a room by pushing gently with first one foot and then the other, at command.

20. Put a wastebasket directly in front of the child. Line up bean-bags or erasers between the basket and the child so that, without changing the place at which he is standing, the child can put the objects into the basket with one hand or the other. His arm movements will have to cross his midline.

21. Roll a ball toward the child, instructing him to kick it back with his right or left foot. Body balance, as well as the right or left response, will be involved. Vary this exercise by having the child lie on his back and kick a ball that hangs from the ceiling.

22. As the child lies (on his back or stomach) on a bench about fourteen inches wide with a sideboard along the legs, direct him to beat either the right or left hand against the side of the bench. (Counting practice can be included here also.)

23. Have the child lie, face down, on the floor. Instruct him to pat the floor with his right or left hand. Do this when his hand is: by his side, extended out from his body, or extended above his head. Repeat, as the child lies on his back.

24. Encourage the child to *do* things with parts of his body:
    a. "Roll up the car window with your left hand."

b. "Touch the wall with your left shoulder."
c. "Make a circle with your left elbow."
d. "Beat this drum with your right wrist."
When possible, have him practice similar manipulation exercises with the feet and legs.

DIRECTIONALITY—A SPATIAL PROJECTION

When the child can transfer his own system of relationships (based on body image and laterality) to the space about him, he develops *directionality*. Note that the reliable transfer depends upon a projection of laterality by the perceptual-motor match, described in Chap. 4. Through directionality, space has meaning, and the child instructs, "Bring me the picture over there to the right!" His environment becomes organized in terms he can comprehend and express correctly, and is no longer cluttered with objects located nowhere. The perception of form is more absolute because parts now have exact locations in relationship to one another, and to the whole form.

Reading reversals and shifts in orientation in reproduction of forms have frequently been noted in the brain damaged. If one does not see a difference between up and down, it is easy to confuse a "b" and a "p." The difficulty is thought of as a failure in the directionality generalization. Exercises to develop directionality include:

1. When riding in a car or walking with the child, ask, "In which direction do we turn to get to where we are going?" The child enthusiastically accepts this game because he likes to know what to anticipate.

2. With the child facing a chalkboard, direct him to draw a line to the right, up, down, etc., varying the directions so that the next command cannot be predicted. Use the dominant hand, then the other, then both hands, increasing the speed of the directions as the child learns. Note that a meaningful drawing is not the desired outcome of this exercise.

3. Instruct: "Touch your left foot with your right hand." "Touch your nose with your right hand." "Put your left hand on my right ear."

4. Have the child describe the exact location of a piece of jewelry on another student.

5. Any child likes to give directions. Have him change roles and direct the teacher or another student, "Touch the red circle at

the left of the chalkboard." It becomes a game to see who interprets the direction first.

6. Have the students close their eyes and place a designated object
within sight in the classroom. Then let them compete to see who
describes the object's exact location.

7. Prepare a lesson sheet by pasting or stamping eight interesting
objects on a piece of paper, arranged so that there are three objects each across the top, sides, and bottom. Place this directly in
front of the child so that the center of the paper corresponds
with his midline. Ask, "What object is located at the bottom,
right of your paper?" or, "What object is at the left, center of
your paper?" When the student can identify the position of
different objects, gradually make all the objects alike on the
paper, such as all triangles. Then instruct, "Put your left hand
on the top, center triangle."

8. As directionality begins to be learned, have the child look at
another person (or doll, animal, picture) and describe whether
a certain body part is on the other person's right or left side.
This is an advanced learning step.

9. Draw designs such as:

FIGURE 5-4

Then ask the child, "Is the circle on the right or left side of the
vertical line?" or, "On which side of the triangle is the vertical
line?"

A TEMPORAL PROJECTION

Another dimension of behavior to be generalized and systematized
(as it has been necessary to do for the spatial dimension) is the *temporal dimension*, which has three aspects: (1) Synchrony; (2) Rhythm;
(3) Sequence.

The basis of temporal judgments originates through *synchrony*
which is a simultaneity in time. A child experiences the meaning of
synchrony as his body parts begin to work together harmoniously.

Muscles move in concert, and the child moves as a unit, one area of the body synchronized with the others.

Having developed a point of origin, the child requires a temporal scale, which must be characterized by stable, equal intervals. *Rhythm* provides such a temporal scale, denoting a patterned movement, with muscles moving alternately or recurrently. Rhythm provides a temporal scale for controlled motor activities through time. Time intervals must be controlled so that they do not run together in a disorganized fashion. Rhythm is *action* and *inhibition*, at ordered intervals. Therefore, a student learns to coordinate in order to make appropriate movements, but he also must be able to *stop*, or inhibit the movement at will. Physical therapy and physical education exercises aid a handicapped child with the control of gross- and fine-motor activities before he can ever begin to sway or to beat time to rhythmic patterns. Then, participation in rhythmic activities offers reinforcement of the body control.

Rhythmic activities help the brain-damaged child develop an *awareness of timing* that is carried over into learning, including counting, writing, and reading. After the child has acquired some sense of timing, he can learn to control temporal intervals so that his rhythm is fast or slow.

Sequence occurs with varied, coordinated motor patterns, and is the ordering of events in time. Obviously, such ordering is difficult or impossible unless there is a temporal scale upon which to superimpose this order. Since much of the behavior of a brain-damaged child is inflexible, it would be assumed that some extremely brain-damaged children are so rigid in their rhythmic associations that they can only sit and rock back and forth in an unchanging time pattern. Other children, who are less handicapped, have great difficulty when they attempt to change a previously learned rhythm pattern. Ask the child to pat his hands on a table-top in a simple left-right pattern. Then request the child to change to other patterns, as a left-left-right pattern or a left-right-right pattern. The task becomes increasingly difficult, or impossible, as the time intervals are quickened.

The *motor-temporal* system must be projected onto outside events just as the *motor-spatial* system is projected onto outside objects. When these systems are effectively used, auditory rhythm develops and speech begins to be rhythmical; the eyes move rhythmically across a page of print; the step-by-step procedures of logical reasoning can be organized in time.

When spatial and temporal systems are adequate, the child can translate activities from one to the other. Consider the task of drawing. The child first looks at the copy and his visual perception gives a simultaneous presentation of the spatial impressions. These impressions may be a series of *events in time* which preserve relationships of the whole. If the form is a square, the child translates four simultaneously presented lines into a series of directional movements performed one at a time, resulting in a square form. Activities to aid in the development of a temporal projection include:

1. TRAMPOLINE ACTIVITIES: For example, the child learns to jump at will. Then he follows one jump with another until he develops a rhythmic pattern. Sequencing begins as the jumping rhythm is correlated with varied body patterns, such as clapping on every third jump.

   Initial trampoline exercises integrate balance in the upright position. This is usually difficult, and it is often necessary for the teacher to get on the trampoline with her student. The basic rhythm of movement on the trampoline should be performed before variations are attempted. When patterning with the legs, it may be necessary for two teachers to work on the trampoline with one student. One teacher manipulates the child's feet while the other holds onto the child's hands, jumping in an upright position. Pattern variations with the legs and arms are learned separately and then combined. Reinforce with verbalization, as "up-down," "in-out," "front-back." If the child is to jump on a trampoline alone, use a very well-protected, large trampoline, or a smaller one perhaps six feet square and only twenty-four inches off the floor.

2. SWIMMING AND WATER ACTIVITIES: The goal of pool activities is not to learn to swim, but rather to provide exercises including synchronized arm and leg motions gradually correlated with one another. The medium of the water allows the child to perform more easily than he does out of water.

3. MUSIC AND ASSOCIATED RHYTHM ACTIVITIES: The continuity of rhythmical patterns in music carries over to assist in the learning of rhythmical motor patterns. For example, the left-right-right hand tapping pattern is easier if the child accompanies his movements with "Peas Porridge Hot—Peas Porridge Cold."

   Introduce songs with a clearly defined beat. Have the child clap or keep time quietly by tapping the finger tips of one hand against the palm of the other. Consider square dancing.

Let the children listen to the ticking of a loud clock. Ask them to tap or to move body parts in time to the ticking. Or verbally imitate the rhythm pattern as the children hold their arms high over their heads and lean far to the left and right at each beat of the "tick-tock." Use a metronone as an auditory stimulus to which the child can respond by physical rhythm patterns. As the children learn one pattern well, vary the metronone speed so that the rhythm awareness is adaptable and generalized.

Consider the rhythm in the syllable emphasis of word construction. Compare words of different syllables, separating them into similar rhythm patterns. Clap to the beat of the syllables:

One Syllable	Two Syllables	Three Syllables
boy	wa-gon	bi-cy-cle
toy	play-ing	po-ta-toes
fly	base-ball	to-ma-to
my	rain-drop	de-li-ver

Let the children think of words familiar to them. Add a musical note to each syllable, and let the children "sing" the word.

4. CHORAL READING ACTIVITIES: These offer a new experience and incorporate the rhythm, physical expression, physical response, verbal expression, listening, memory, and fun activities of music itself. Through choral reading, children share words, rhythm, and expression in ways that they are unable to do by just talking. Most children participating in choral reading must have some verbal ability, but some can participate using *motions* or rhythm *instruments*.

Begin with rhymes and repetitive phrases:

Teacher: Little Boy Blue, come blow your horn;
Children: Blow, blow, blow
Teacher: The sheep's in the meadow, the cow's in the corn.
Children: Oh, Oh, Oh
Teacher: Where's the little boy that looks after the sheep?
Children: Ho, ho, ho
Teacher: He's under the hay-cock, fast asleep.
Children: Go, go, go.

Next, proceed to nursery rhymes:

a. Divide a class into groups, and alternate the lines of poetry

between the groups, occasionally having them recite together:

1st Group: Little Miss Muffet sat on a tuffet
2nd Group: Eating her curds and whey
1st Group: Along came a spider
2nd Group: And sat down beside her
All: And frightened Miss Muffet away!

Be sure the pronunciation and meaning of each word are
understood. Teach the children to speak with expression so
that their words have distinct sounds. Be sure that some
phrases are emphasized, and that quiet and low tones are
regulated.

b. Select *solo* parts for particular students. A favorite is:

All: Pussy cat, pussy cat, where have you been?
Solo: I've been to London to see the queen.
All: Pussy cat, pussy cat, what did you do there?
Solo: I frightened a little mouse under the chair.

c. Select only two students to present a reading:

Solo I: Jack, be nimble
Solo II: Jack, be quick
Both: Jack, jump over the candlestick!

Proceed to original rhymes with motions. If the class is capable
of doing so, put choral readings and motions together. For example, in the following, the children clap their hands as they
say "dogs" or "frogs," but at the word "and" they turn their
hands palm side up:

Dogs, dogs, dogs and dogs
Frogs, frogs, frogs and frogs!

Ask the children to make up their own words that rhyme and
to make up simple motions to go with them.

chapter 6

The Developmental
Stages of Learning

Six general stages of learning are recognized, in sequential order: (1) A Gross-Motor Stage; (2) A Motor-Perceptual Stage; (3) A Perceptual-Motor Stage; (4) A Perceptual Stage; (5) A Perceptual-Conceptual Stage; and (6) A Conceptual Stage. The *order* of the stages is more important than *when* each occurs. They are hierarchical, building upon themselves in a related series, although it is recognized that there is some overlapping. Perceptual-motor learning is incomplete if the child's gross-motor learning has been distorted. Likewise, conceptual learning is hindered if areas of gross-motor and perceptual-motor learning have been omitted. Dunsing confirms:

> We hold that the most basic component of readiness development is motor. Perceptual information is crucial but it must be organized in relation to the child's early exploratory activity, and such organization will occur only insofar as the child's motor exploration is consistent and organized. The child's earliest motor explorations are organized in terms of his relationship to gravity and consist of patterns of posture and balance movements which tend to orient him to the earth's surface and to the object world. As his movement activities become more highly organized, he is increasingly able to structure his perceptual input so as to make sense of it. We believe that cognitive organization is no more sound than the perceptual organization which underlies it. The only way a child can veridicate

his conceptualizations is through a well-established perceptual structure which is organized, in turn, upon a solid motor base.[1]

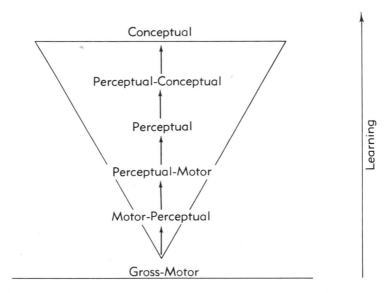

FIGURE 6-1.   The developmental stages of learning are hierarchical.

A GROSS-MOTOR STAGE

The child's first attempts to organize his environment occur as he
maneuvers and receives sensory information. For example, the child
crawls along the floor and bumps into a wall. In the gross-motor stage
we are not interested in movement per se, but *in motor activities for
their contribution to the development of information.* Motor control,
for example, is important for accurate kinesthetic information. For a
large number of children, the learning difficulty begins at this early
motor stage. A lack of control causes the child to stumble, to spill
things, or to be slow in learning to manipulate his hands. One child
complained, "I can't keep up with my feet!" The child learns to use
motor responses to accomplish certain goals, but brain damage may
prohibit him from expanding motor responses to form the *basis of*

---

[1]"Readiness Training," Position paper, Workshop on Perceptual Motor Dysfunction, American Orthopsychiatric Association, April, 1966.

information gathering. He is in trouble because he has not developed a flexible motor interaction with his environment; he is learning a *motor skill* and not a *motor pattern.*

A *motor skill* is an act performed with a high degree of precision, and only limited variation is possible. A *motor pattern* is coordinated motor behavior composed of a combination of movements, adapted to serve a purpose. It is a motor generalization, allowing for a great degree of variability. Motor patterns are essential for information gathering at a very basic stage of the child's development. In dealing with minimally brain-damaged children it is frequently observed that specific skills, such as walking, can be taught with little difficulty. Patterns of movement, however, become much harder to achieve, particularly when there are alterations in the task, or in the environment surrounding the task. Since many children find the motor learning required for a motor pattern difficult, they stop with a motor skill. They require additional help and learning experiences to continue motor learning until a level is reached permitting the use of movement skills within motor patterns.

Four educationally significant motor patterns are discussed: (1) Locomotion; (2) Balance and Maintenance of Posture; (3) Contact; and (4) Receipt and Propulsion. All of these motor patterns should provide *consistent* and *extensive* interaction with the environment, or interpretation will lack stability and completeness. The patterns should be so well established that the child is free to direct his attention to the *purpose* for the movement rather than to the motor acts themselves. These patterns should also be variable, permitting complex manipulations in search of information.

LOCOMOTION

The locomotor skills are motor activities which move the body through space: walking, running, skipping, hopping, rolling, etc. Walking, then, is *part of a locomotor pattern*, within which specific activities can be used alternately or in combination. The brain-damaged child develops a walking skill by maintaining an upright position while putting one foot in front of the other; this process allows him to move. However, most of his attention must be devoted to *what* part moves and *how.* If he encounters an obstacle, he cannot veer around it or step over it because these adjustments involve greater shifting of direction and variation in movement sequences than his limited skill permits.

BALANCE AND MAINTENANCE OF POSTURE

A well-organized system of the three Euclidean dimensions of space is necessary for the child's organization of his environment. His own center of gravity becomes the point of origin for spatial orientation, and relationship to gravity is achieved through the motor pattern of balance and posture. By adjusting his body to the force of gravity, the child identifies the direction of the line of gravity and maintains this constant throughout his interaction with the world. Through a dynamic relationship to gravity, a continuous awareness of its direction can be maintained. (Exercises to aid balance are given in Chap. 5.)

CONTACT

The skills of the contact pattern are motor activities by which objects are manipulated, such as *reaching*, *grasping*, and *releasing*. With these, the child investigates similarities and differences, *reaching out* to make contact with objects, maintaining this contact by *grasping*, and terminating the contact by *releasing*. From knowledge so gained, form perception and figure-ground relationships develop.

RECEIPT AND PROPULSION

Movements in space are investigated by receipt and propulsion. Using receipt skills, the child makes contact with a moving object. This includes not only the pursuit of the object, but also the interposition of the body or body parts in the path of the moving object, as in catching. The skills of propulsion involve activities by which movement is imparted to an object, including throwing, batting, and the more continuous skills of pushing and pulling.

A MOTOR-PERCEPTUAL STAGE

Motor explorations are still the controlling aspect at this stage, but the child begins to move more efficiently by using data he perceives, or has perceived, during motor explorations. For example, the child no longer bumps into a wall when he crawls across the room because he sees it is there and interprets what it means. A child may touch an object, insisting, "I want to feel how it looks."

A PERCEPTUAL-MOTOR STAGE

In the perceptual-motor stage, the child acquires ability to *control* his maneuvering in terms of perceptual information. Maneuvering and the perception reinforce each other, enabling the child to stabilize an accurate impression. This stabilization, the *perceptual-motor match*, is described in detail in Chap. 4. If this match does not occur, the child lives in two different worlds: (1) the perceptual world in which he sees, hears, tastes, smells, and feels, and (2) a motor world in which he responds. When these two worlds are not matched, the child gains conflicting information and is constantly confused by two sources of information that are not identical.

A PERCEPTUAL STAGE

In the perceptual stage, the child manipulates one perception against another, without the necessity of motor intervention. The child notices that objects have perceptual similarities, and is able, for example, to sort cardboard squares, circles, and triangles by simply *looking* at them; it is not necessary for him to feel them to differentiate. Perceptual discrimination can be practiced and learned.

AUDITORY DISCRIMINATION EXERCISES

1. Have a blindfolded child identify: the individual voices of his classmates, which musical instrument is being played, whether a high or low note is sounded on the piano, whether the eraser or lead end of the pencil is tapping a table.

2. Have the child identify rhyming words.

3. Modify "Simon Says" by *always* saying (and never omitting) the words "Simon says." The children will have enough to think about just following the directions, without having to consider how the directions are stated. Gradually speed up the directions.

4. Have the child imitate sounds. (Include syllable combinations that are not words.) Collect pictures of objects to be identified

with words beginning with letter sounds. Many of these pictures are available from speech therapists. Have the child distinguish between sounds that are similar.

5. Talk about "what things say": the "drip-drip" of a water faucet, the train wheels going "clickety-clack," the train whistle saying "toot-toot," and the "tap-tap-tap-tap" of a hammer as it pounds on a nail.

6. Speak in a sentence, pronouncing one word incorrectly. Have the child "discover" the word and say it to you correctly.

AUDITORY MEMORY AND SEQUENCING EXERCISES

1. Have the child listen to the beat of a tom-tom or drum and then copy the pattern by clapping or hitting on a table.

2. Read a simple paragraph: "The big, brown dog had a very little bone. He dug a big hole and buried the bone. He filled up the hole with dirt. After that he wagged his tail because he was happy." (The complexity of the sentences should vary with the child's ability to comprehend. Start with paragraphs from a preprimer and proceed through a reading series.) Then ask, "What did the dog have?" "What did the dog do with the bone?" "Was the dog sad or happy?" "What color was the dog?" Eventually, the child retells events to the teacher in story form.

3. Have the child recall nursery rhymes, and then simple poetry.

4. Have the child recall and then follow verbal directions. Increase the number of directions as the child learns.

5. As the child listens to a story that is told, read, or recorded, have him use the flannelboard to illustrate what he hears.

6. Have the child recognize whether auditory stimuli are fast or slow.

7. Have the child tell you the time by listening to the number of times the clock strikes.

8. Tap the table with a stick or similar object, instructing, "*Listen, watch*, and *count out loud* while I tap on the table." Listening is reinforced by the seeing and the speaking. Ask, "How many times was the table tapped?" Next, take away the visual reinforcement. Instruct, "Close your eyes and count out loud while I tap the table." When identification is mastered by the combina-

tion of speech and listening, omit speech and ask for recognition while the child *watches* and *listens*. For the final step, have the child close his eyes and *listen* only. Use all of the above steps while playing a note on the piano, beating a drum, tapping a glass with a spoon, and tapping a xylophone.

9. Say letters, words, or numbers in sequential order, asking the child to repeat them when you finish the sequence. Next, after stating a sequence, restate it, *leaving out* a unit. Ask, "What did I leave out?" Next, restate a sequence, *adding* a unit. Ask, "What did I add?" Finally, ask the child to repeat a sequence *in reverse*.

VISUAL DISCRIMINATION EXERCISES

1. Provide printed exercises in which the child finds like objects (such as circles) that are a part of a total picture.

2. Provide printed exercises in which the child finds "hidden objects" in a picture.

3. Teach the child to estimate the distance between objects (spatial discrimination). Say, "Place these as far apart as those." A harder task requires the child to place two objects as far apart as the length of a desk or the width of a doorway.

4. Have the child match silhouettes of an object to the actual picture of that object.

5. Use "what's-missing pictures" that require careful observation of details. For example, a picture of a child may show that he is ready to play in the snow, but has forgotten to put on one sock and shoe.

6. Act out a situation and ask the child to tell you what you have done wrong. For example say, "I am at a movie," and sit down in a chair and close your eyes. Or say, "I am eating soup," and pantomime eating with a knife and fork.

7. Have the child imitate movement patterns. (Refer to *The Slow Learner in the Classroom*, p. 131.)

8. Identify many objects and their colors.

9. Convey some idea of the measurements of objects. Exhibit two or more boxes, bottles, toy animals, pencils, or apples, and ask the children to compare them in size. Sometimes use two objects of identical size.

VISUAL MEMORY AND SEQUENCING EXERCISES

1. Ask the children to survey the teacher or another student. Have that person leave the room and add or subtract an article of clothing, or change his attire in some way. Give a prize to the first child who notices what has changed.

2. Provide a memory game consisting of sets of matching pictures. After a series of the pictures is turned face down, have the child recall *where* he saw a picture, and then have him put the matching picture with it.

3. Hold up one picture. Take it away, and then show the child several pictures. Ask, "Which one have you just seen?" At first, there should be gross differences in the pictures (boy, girl, man). As the child learns, the differences can be more subtle (all boys).

4. Have the children look around the room. Then say, "Now close your eyes and tell me what you saw."

5. Stimulate the child's visual recall by asking, "What did you eat for lunch?" "What color are your bedroom walls?"

6. Help the child to transpose visual patterns, such as:

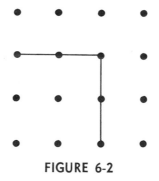

FIGURE 6-2

Also refer to the form-board patterns in the Appendix.

7. Put a gradually increasing number of objects on a tray.
    a. Take the tray away, and ask the child to name the objects.
    b. Remove an object, and ask for the name of the one that is missing.
    c. Add an object, and ask for the name of the addition.

    d. Change the order of the objects. Have the child put them as they were.

This exercise can also be done with shapes on a flannelboard.

8. Have one student look around the room to see who is present. Then have him close his eyes while one student leaves. Can he name who has left?

A PERCEPTUAL-CONCEPTUAL STAGE

As the child deals with perceptual similarities, a concept begins to develop from percepts. For example, the child now knows that a square and a triangle are different *because* one has four sides and the other has three. (See Chap. 7.)

A CONCEPTUAL STAGE

In the conceptual stage, the child learns to group and to relate perceptual data into meaningful generalizations which he can use in the future. For example, he knows that a circle can be used for a wheel, and why. Conceptual thinking may be taught by using concrete perceptual-motor information, but the concern with the conceptual stage is that its development cannot be physically manipulated as easily as in the preceding developmental stages. The actual relationship of some information requires an element of abstract visualization.

chapter 7

Conceptualization

Conceptualization is "relating what is perceived," or "the ability to identify a stimulus and to relate the resulting percepts." To relate is to connect by meaning. A *percept* is the identification of a stimulus. Conceptualizing begins with confrontation by a stimulus. The stimulus is identified and becomes a meaningful percept through the cyclical thought (stimulus-response) processing described in Chap. 4. As the child relates his perceptual data through similarities and differences, he forms *concepts*.

Many brain-damaged children identify a stimulus with a conditioned reaction, but they do not relate identifications. These children are "perceptualizing," not conceptualizing. Brain-damaged children vary greatly in their ability to perceptualize, or to conceptualize, or to do a little of both.

Conceptualization is a step-by-step, hierarchical process. First, a stimulus is identified so that it becomes a meaningful *percept;* second, percepts are related to form *concepts;* third, past and present percepts and concepts are related and projected to form *future concepts;* fourth, future concepts are related to form *predictions;* fifth, predictions are related to form the ultimate in conceptualization—PLANNING.

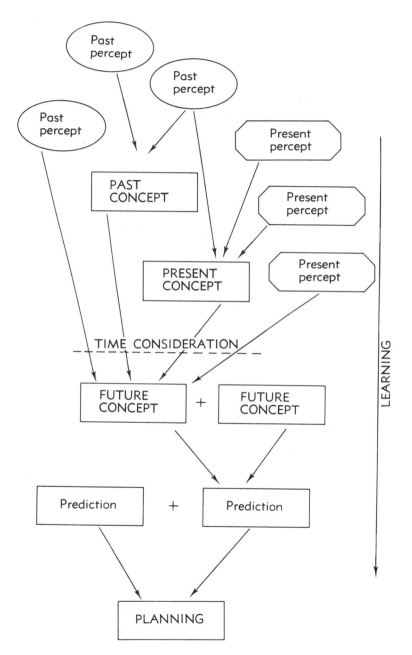

FIGURE 7-1. A diagrammatic summary of the hierarchical development of conceptualization.

RELATING SPACE AND TIME
TO CONCEPTUALIZATION

The relationship between percepts is in (1) space, (2) time, or (3) space *and* time ("use").

THE SPACE FACTOR

"Long and short," "big and little," "here and there," "beside and behind" are all examples of percepts related in space. Accurate relating of these comparisons is directly dependent upon the projection of spatial relationships. (Chapter 6 correlates laterality and directionality with spatial data.)

THE TIME FACTOR

Time is a longitudinal factor enabling a child to perceive a *sequence of percepts*. Brain damage makes it difficult or impossible to organize sequential data. A relationship of present and past percepts may be sufficient for the present. But what of the future? The child must be taught that present data can be *projected* to form "predictions." Relating predictions helps to *plan ahead*.

USE—INVOLVING SPACE AND TIME

"Use" designates a series of spatial relationships in time. Hitting a nail with a hammer forcibly brings together and separates two objects in space over a period of time. When an object is "thrown," the distance between the object and the person throwing is quickly increased, during a period of time. Therefore, *relating percepts by space, time, and use is teaching the development of a concept:*

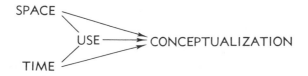

FIGURE 7-2

READINESS ABILITIES DIRECTLY AFFECTING
CONCEPTUALIZATION

Conceptualization demands readiness for both the student *and* the teacher:

1. Confirm the efficient and accurate use of the child's sensory mechanisms, so that his information is valid. Since many handicapped children avoid looking at or listening to a stimulus, these abilities should precede or coincide with the teaching of identification. (Refer to Chap. 4 for elaboration regarding response to stimuli, and to Chap. 6 regarding auditory and visual reception.)

2. Teach each student to have an organized awareness of himself as the only stable point of reference for discerning relationships. (Refer to Chap. 5.) A percept is directly dependent upon self-organization and functioning of perceptual mechanisms:

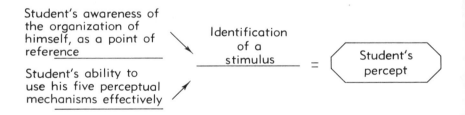

FIGURE 7-3

3. Present perceptual stimuli in a meaningful way, according to the learning capacities of the individual. Use appropriate auditory, visual, and tactile-kinesthetic methods. (Refer to Chap. 4.)

4. Since *remembering* must be *taught* to some brain-damaged children, provide exercises to aid recall. Then, for conceptualization, the student is better prepared to relate what he *has perceived* to what *is perceived*, or *will be perceived*.

5. Expose the student to an abundance of stimuli to avoid a rigidity of perceptual data and to accumulate a wealth of basic information. A student may surprise you by referring later to a stimulus you thought he did not notice.

6. Plan lessons for teaching an organized set of relationships—similarities and differences. Lessons should proceed in a methodical, hierarchical way.

STEP I—BUILDING A VOCABULARY
THROUGH IDENTIFICATION

Vocabulary-building includes four types of identification: (1) animate objects, including people; (2) inanimate objects; (3) places and situations; (4) abstract terms. Include *controlling the child's reaction* to other persons, objects, and places while he is learning about them. For example, "people" *and* "getting along with people" must be taught together. If accepted reactions are learned simultaneously with meeting the new situations, an *associated impression* is made, and the child's behavior and understanding improve, as well as his vocabulary.

IDENTIFYING ANIMATE OBJECTS

Because of an inability to speak, to move about, or to react appropriately, a handicapped child has a limited exposure to cooperative play, which directly restricts his perception of similarities and differences that identify people. Therefore, a concentrated effort, with discretion, must expose the child to a variety of personalities. Socialization in a classroom at an early age provides friends to identify. Other identifications are provided by:

1. guest speakers, particularly those relating well to children by presenting music, stories, or collections;

2. pictures of people, that are well-defined views with a plain background. If a child is having difficulty with figure-ground relationships, a complicated background adds to his confusion. Use magazines and books to make collections of all types of people. Use transparent slides, moving pictures, and paintings;

3. field trips, including visits to stores, libraries, radio stations, police and fire stations;

4. social and study situations, such as camping, visits with friends and relatives, parties, church school, and picnics.

Many beneficial classroom-inspired projects can relate to animals: hatch eggs in an incubator; raise polywogs (if possible, allow the children to go to a stream to get the polywogs); visit a zoo; go fishing; visit an aquarium. Elementary science books give numerous suggestions for learning about animals. Identification of animals, as identification of people, opens up a new, delightful world for a handicapped child.

IDENTIFYING INANIMATE OBJECTS

Identification of objects is one of the easiest lessons to present in a classroom because materials are concrete and unlimited. Watch carefully to see HOW the child learns about an object. Does he remember best by seeing it, feeling it, or hearing it called by name? This gives clues for presenting other materials to that same child. To present objects:

1. Provide objects in the classroom. The child can *participate* in teaching and learning if he brings an object about which he "tells" as he "shows" it to classmates. Bring a "surprise sack" containing new objects. Instilling an interest in objects is the beginning of childhood collections and hobbies. It is a fortunate teacher or parent who discovers the child's pockets full of all sorts of objects, for this is proof that the child is beginning to *observe* and to react to his environment.

2. Show transparent slides and movies.

3. Look at pictures in magazines, newspapers, and books and discuss them.

4. Discover associations on *excursions*. A picnic, for example, is identified with a basket, potato salad, beans, lemonade, etc.

5. *Act out* the use of an object. Examples include a ball, screwdriver, drum, telephone, bicycle, piano, and trumpet. Both the acting and the guessing are fun.

IDENTIFYING PLACES AND SITUATIONS

In order to identify a place or situation as a *whole*, including the various *parts*, it is necessary to consider *several* objects and persons at one time and to comprehend the relationship between them. This is more complex than identification of a single object or person. Ask *why* a particular object is present: "Why is this suitcase in the train station?"

As the student learns to relate comparisons, he appraises a total situation. For example, he looks at a person standing beside a table and describes two *spatial* relationships: the person is beside the table; and the person is taller than the table. The situation is more complex if the person is doing something to an object, such as leaning against a building, as this also involves an *action relationship in time*. Teach the child to perceive:

> There is a boy.
> There is a building.
> The boy is leaning against the building.
> The boy is shorter than the building.
> The building cannot move, but the boy can.
> The building is hard.
> The boy eats, but the building doesn't.
> The boy has hair, but the building doesn't.

The best teaching technique for learning about places is to have the child *experience* what happens there.

DENNIS THE MENACE   By Hank Ketcham

"Boy! You sure can't tell how deep a puddle is from the top, can you?"

© The Hall Syndicate, Inc. T.M. ®

FIGURE 7-4

Because of the difficulty of taking a class of handicapped children on a field trip, the burden of offering numerous experiences to the child lies with his parents. Classroom teaching can then *reinforce* the child's experience by relating pictures, stories, and drawings, or by introducing circumstances similar to those with which the child is familiar. For example, if a child has visited a train station, he should relate this to what he would see if he went to an airport. Identification of situations includes a boy feeding a dog, people laughing, a baby crying, and a man driving a car. Check the ability to recognize a situation by directing, "Show me how to look tired," or "Show me what a baby does when he is sleepy."

IDENTIFYING ABSTRACT TERMS

Abstractions include such words as love, hate, friendship, wish, patience, sadness, funny, right, and wrong. To identify these:

1. *Explain the abstract in terms of the concrete.* For example, for a "wish" teach "A wish is something you ask to have happen." Have the child make a wish that *can* happen, such as, "I wish a book were in my hand." Then put the book into his hands, asking, "Did your wish come true? This is what you *wished* for."

2. *Point out the relationship of the abstract word to another the child already knows.* "Patience" means "to wait." As one mother related, "John came to me when I was helping David with his tie. He asked me to do something for him. I answered, 'Wait until I help David. Sit in the chair and be patient.' John flung himself against the wall. I led him back to the chair, explaining, 'Patience means to wait. You wait here and be patient until I finish with David.' John waited as directed. Finally, I turned to him and expressed my pleasure, saying, 'Good, you were patient. Now you may come here.' John beamed and exclaimed, 'I waited! I am learning to be patient.'" The mother had deliberately caused her child to experience the similarity between waiting and patience; for a normal child, a verbal explanation alone might have been enough.

   Patience can be taught by *timing*. Expect the child to be quiet for gradually increasing periods of time. Use a bell or other concrete notification to indicate when the waiting is over.

   Relate patience to calendar studies. Subtract days from the calendar prior to an event in the future. Or teach patience by having the child wait until the hands of a clock reach a designated time.

Teach patience, for example, while the child is helping to get breakfast for his family. If he is impatient and rushes too fast, eggs will break, milk will spill, and food will burn. Let the child experiment to see for himself that this is true! Then help him proceed slowly.

STEP II–RELATING TWO OR MORE PERCEPTS TO FORM A CONCEPT

We are continually exposed to stimuli to be identified, as percepts A through E in Fig. 7-5. We take note of, or "catalogue," these percepts until there is reason to relate one with another, as percepts B and E are related to form the concept BE. Under different circumstances, we may relate percepts B and D.

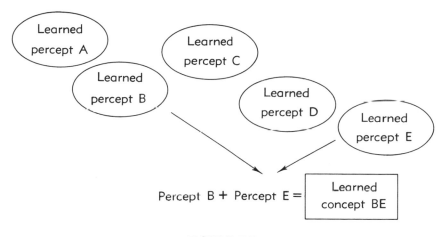

Percept B + Percept E = Learned concept BE

FIGURE 7-5

In the diagram, "learned" is specified because, without special teaching help, a brain-damaged individual is left to flounder with percepts that seldom become meaningful to him. He is unable to generalize from his percepts. Little wonder that his actions often do not make sense! When a child finally relates his percepts he moves from a haphazard world into a more comfortable, organized, meaningful existence. Relating two specific percepts is illustrated in Fig. 7-6, p. 84.

The *approach* to teaching conceptualization is exact. But many words can be related by different reasons. Also, *more* than two percepts can be related. At this stage of learning, the teaching of conceptualiza-

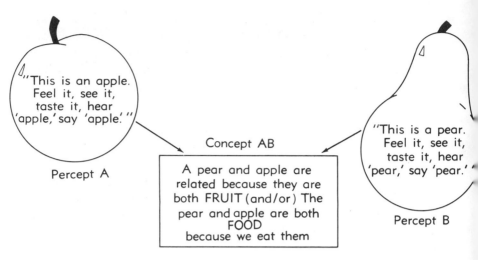

"This is an apple. Feel it, see it, taste it, hear 'apple,' say 'apple.'"

Percept A

Concept AB

A pear and apple are related because they are both FRUIT (and/or) The pear and apple are both FOOD because we eat them

"This is a pear. Feel it, see it, taste it, hear 'pear,' say 'pear.'"

Percept B

FIGURE 7-6.   Relating percepts to form a concept. (Refer to p. 83.)

tion is limited by the *total number* and *accuracy* of the student's percepts.

Sorting, sequencing, categorizing, and comparing overlap in function. Items are classified according to a specific relationship to another item. In deliberately using these four methods, the selection of the identifying *characteristics* of the item involved is as important as the teaching technique that is used. To identify the item, the child *perceives the characteristics* which become *percepts*. The identification of "a small stone," for example, involves two percepts: "This is a stone," and "This is small." Therefore, when asking a brain-damaged child to sort, sequence, categorize, or compare, consider that there are three types of percepts, listed in order of increasing difficulty:

1.   *concrete* percepts;
2.   percepts identifying *use;*
3.   *abstract* percepts.

Concrete percepts can be immediately perceived, and a child distinguishes one from another by feeling, seeing, hearing, smelling, or tasting. Have the child participate in the following activities involving concrete percepts:

1.   Taste dill pickles and sugar, and tell which is sweet, or sour.
2.   Study the relationship of "short and long" by manipulating

lines of varying lengths such as those cut out of paper, wood, or cardboard. Paste them on paper according to their size. Draw lines of varying lengths. Compare short and long objects.

3. Compare "big and little" by manipulations suggested in (2). Sort big and little seeds into piles, or use them to create a design by alternating them on outlines of geometric forms.

4. Compare a fish and giraffe. Compare a pen and a pin.

5. Sort silverware into sections of the silverware drawer.

6. Cut a size-series of circles, squares, and triangles out of tackboard, first making the same shapes the same color, and later varying their color. Arrange them in descending order according to size. Note that the ability to arrange one thing after another precedes skills such as spelling or writing.

7. Provide "heavy and light" articles to be sorted. Pour varying amounts of cement into cans of the same size. Cover the open end of the cans so that the child cannot see the difference in the amount of cement. When the student can easily sort the cans into two groups according to weight, introduce cans of intermediate weight. This technique promotes the beginning realization that weight is not always determined by size.

8. Sort shapes by whether they go into round, square, or triangular holes.

9. Sort poker chips, pegs, blocks, or paper chips according to color.

10. Arrange color chips in a series, according to the intensity gradations of the same color. (Obtain these chips from paint stores.)

11. Make a puzzle by painting a design of a basic shape on wood. Then cut plain strips of wood which can be laid on the design in proper size sequence. Vary this technique by adding colored stripes to the shape painted on the wood. Paint the puzzle strips the same color as the area on which they belong.

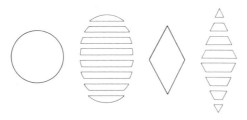

FIGURE 7-7

12. Start a collection of boxes or bottles with tops, preferably with no variations in color. Determine which bottom goes with which top, and arrange them in order of size.

13. Use varieties of objects whose parts *fit into* one another, such as a series of boxes gradually decreasing in size.

14. Make scrapbooks: "Round Things," "Red Things," "Big and Little Things."

15. Collect objects and sort them into appropriate piles, such as buttons, sticks, and pebbles.

Relating concrete percepts helps the child to be increasingly aware of the characteristics of the people and things in his environment, observing: "The pencil is smaller than I am. It is made of wood and I am not. It doesn't have ears, but I do." "This fire engine is painted red; I am not painted, but I have skin. The fire engine is bigger than I am. It can't talk, but I can."

It should be understood that there is a big difference between the child's ability to sort according to characteristics and his ability to *describe something verbally*. In the first case, the stimuli are present to be perceived, but in the second, the child must *remember* what he has previously perceived and then he must verbalize this recall. To help a child with verbalization, encourage him to *convince* you about an arrangement. For example, in a series as:

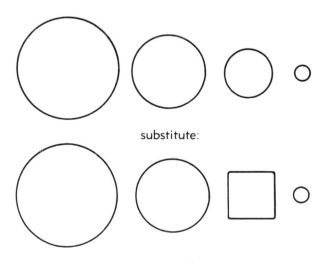

substitute:

FIGURE 7-8

Ask, "Why is the second series wrong?"

Even if the child does not describe, he still may be able to answer such questions as: Is a girl smaller than a woman? Do fish fly? Who has more legs, you or a rabbit?

The *use* of an object involves more than immediately perceived identifying characteristics. Use consists of percepts related in space and time. Therefore, when we require sorting, sequencing, categorizing, or comparing according to use, we require a more difficult task than when we ask for identification by concrete observation. Have the child perform the following exercises:

1. Sort pictures of articles of clothing into piles according to their use for weather conditions, sports, or occasions.

2. Underline the similar objects:
    apple   house   wagon   pear

3. Decide which can be eaten:
    banana   typewriter   apple   key

4. Play games of association lotto.

5. State which word does not relate to the others:
    man   boy   car   woman

6. Make scrapbooks: "How to be a good friend," "How we hold things together" (as with glue, nails, staples, pins, tapes, or by sewing), "How we travel," "Signs of spring."

7. Sort "what we want to keep" and "what we want to throw away" at the end of a busy day. This categorizes articles according to their usefulness.

8. Observe pictures showing similar functions and describe *why* the functions are similar. Later, select from a group of pictures the one that does not belong: a man building a toy, a boy building a hot-rod, a carpenter nailing boards on a house, and a boy riding his bike.

9. Present related tasks in the classroom: drawing shapes on the chalkboard, pounding a nail with a hammer, and pounding pegs on a pounding board. Identify the task that is different from the rest. Explain why.

A child does not suddenly switch from thinking in the concrete to thinking in the abstract. Experimentation may be *partially concrete* and *partially abstract*. This "concrete-abstract" area warrants careful consideration because it is an area in which the brain damaged can begin to participate in the abstract, while still depending upon the concrete. Activities involving transitional considerations include:

1. Have the child draw a triangle by connecting three dots. Ask how the triangle can be made larger.

2. Have the child make a square, with pegs, around the outside of a pegboard. Instruct, "Make a square *inside* this one."

3. Have the child build a fence around little animals.

4. Hold up cards, directing "The red dot means to hold up your right arm, and the green dot means to hold up your left arm."

Activities involving abstract comparisons include:

1. Have the child sort pictures according to whether they are funny or sad.

2. Have the child find pictures where someone is doing something wrong.

3. Ask the child to tell about times when people have been honest.

ANALYSIS

In the previous exercises where different types of percepts have been related to form a total concept, the student has gone through the process of putting parts (percepts) together to make a whole. The student comprehends the whole better because he understands the parts. *Teach the child how to reverse this technique.* Let him take a whole and break it down into its parts, and then put it together again. Have him look at a picture or a situation and *analyze* it: "Why is it winter?" Have the child perform the following activities:

1. Read a story, then reconstruct it in pictures or by verbalization. Or, look at some pictures and then make up a story with them.

2. Take a miniature town apart, discussing why each part was there in the first place. Then rebuild the town, explaining why certain buildings are grouped together.

3. Take apart toys that come in sections, then put the toys together again.

4. Roll modeling clay into a ball. Slice it, then put the ball back together again.

5. Look at an object from one angle, then show pictures of other views. Ask the child to identify the object from all views.

STEP III—RELATING A LEARNED CONCEPT WITH A LEARNED PERCEPT

Conceptualization can be developed by relating one or more learned concepts with one or more new percepts. The process is illustrated using Percept C and Concept AB:

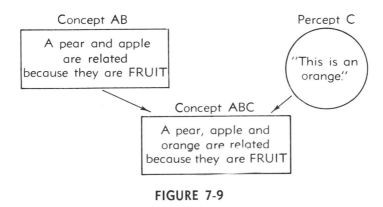

FIGURE 7-9

STEP IV- RELATING SIMPLE CONCEPTS TO FORM MORE COMPLEX CONCEPTS

Conceptualization advances beyond the level of relating percepts to the relating of concepts as illustrated in Fig. 7-10, p. 90.

There are brain-damaged children who will never relate stimuli automatically. But for many there can be a carry-over from the *learned* to the automatic relating of identified stimuli. Awareness of the beginning ability to relate stimuli occurs as the child exclaims, "Why Sally's dog looks like Billy's. They both have black fur!" Or, "Your hat is just like my mother's. They both have pretty flowers!"

A child continually asks "WHEN," because his percepts in space are unrelated by *continuity in time*. Then the child persists, "When am I going to camp?" "When did we see Joey?" "When did Billy hit me?" The child needs help relating the past, present, and future.

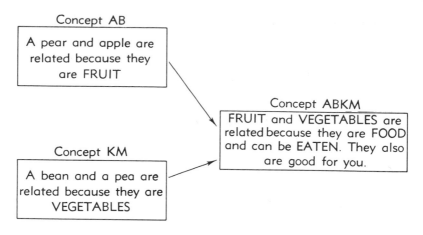

FIGURE 7-10.   Relating concepts. (Refer to p. 89.)

STEP V—RELATING THE PAST, PRESENT, AND FUTURE

A present (immediate) percept is one being learned NOW: "This is an apple." A past percept is one learned previously. It is still stated, "This is an apple," but it has been learned BEFORE NOW. Today the child knows that this is an apple because the stimulus persists in his mind. He does not need to relate the percept to the fact that he perceived it before now. At this stage of learning, TODAY the child looks at a symbolic representation of what he has previously learned; he compares the two and learns that they are the same.

Relating a past percept to another requires that the teacher keep a record of what percepts a child has learned in past days; these are then related to what the child perceives NOW. (Note: The ability to remember relates directly to how effectively the child relates to the past, and "the past" can mean any length of time before now. Therefore, when teaching, consider that there may be a direct ratio between "how long ago the stimulus occurred" and "how well the past stimulus can be related to the present.") An oversimplified lesson plan for relating past percepts might be:

October 1—Teach percept of an apple;
October 2—Teach percept of a pear;
October 3—Teach concept of FRUIT.

Classroom projects include:

1. Refer to the exercises concerning ANALYSIS given in this chapter. Use these same lessons again, but introduce a time factor, so that "taking apart" or "putting together" have a significant interval of time between them.

2. Show pictures presenting cause and effect. The student must "think back" regarding why or when the problem occurred. Ask, "How did this nail get through this board?" "Why is this tree lying on the ground?" "Why does this dog have a bandage on his foot?" "What happened to this wrecked car?"

A future (predictive) concept is projected AHEAD, and formed by (1) a percept known now, related to (2) the percepts, acknowledging the passing of time. *By definition, a "future percept" is not possible because the percept cannot exist without considering time.* An example of a future concept is: This object will be an apple whenever I see it. A cell assembly (refer to Chap. 4) is established including the present and past percepts. These are related to one another, and from them another concept (present or future) evolves. Therefore, the future concept is a projection based on past and present percepts and/or concepts, with appropriate elaborations and modifications occurring as there is FEEDBACK to the original cell assembly. The future concept evolves with a flexibility not found in a past or present percept. Examples of future concepts include:

> Tomorrow our teacher will be Mrs. Jones.
> Tommy will have red hair tomorrow.
> I will be living in the same house next Tuesday.

All of these are based upon concrete realities *which a child can observe to be true TODAY*, or which the child *learned* were true BEFORE TODAY. Tomorrow, the child can *check* his future observations by returning to his concrete observations of the previous day. He learns that he predicted correctly.

Normal adults recall that, as children, they had many opportunities to question their predictions:

> "If I hit him, will he hit me back?"
> "If I step on this crack, will it break my mother's back?"
> "If I run too hard, will I get out of breath?"
> "If I step on this bug, will it kill the bug?"

But how often does a brain-damaged child have the same opportunities to experiment with similar questions? Through opportunities to test his predictions a child discovers his ability to look ahead, and he becomes more comfortable because his environment can be anticipated:

1. Play "pretend games" as a type of predictive activity. The children can pretend they are getting ready for a birthday party, and act out the preparations and party. They *anticipate* their next moves.

2. Emphasize the cause and effect relationship of discipline: "If you touch this hot stove you will be burned."

3. "Check ahead on the calendar" to furnish an easy way of anticipating in the classroom. Cover the date with an object, so that the student can *see*, "Tomorrow is next, and the date will be—."

4. Encourage *guessing* as the children learn that they cannot *always* predict about tomorrow: "Mrs. Jones is wearing a yellow scarf today. Who can predict what Mrs. Jones will wear tomorrow?"

5. Teach the child how to anticipate a task. For cleaning a room, have him select which areas to clean as well as what tools to use.

6. Let the children plan pictures to create. To make a big American flag, have them decide how many red and white paper strips and white stars to cut out; plan the spatial relationships of the flag's parts; and then plan the time relationships of how long it will take to complete the flag. Have the children study a real flag before they plan their own.

7. Provide puzzles to put together. Select puzzles of pictures with definite forms, so that the children must *predict* ahead of time in order to put the correct piece next. If the form is a person, have the children predict which body part is put next to make the person "whole."

8. Have the children write letters, and project thoughts to write, considering news and what the recipient would like to hear.

9. Have the children *anticipate* trips. Whether a trip to the store, to the dentist, to grandmother's, or to a party, a child needs to anticipate what his experience may be. *Rehearsals help him to be more secure when the actual experience occurs.*

10. Show pictures from which the child can make up stories. He derives the facts from his ability to anticipate and to imagine.

11. Consider action predictions:
    "If I throw this egg, what will happen?"
    "Can we travel in a teapot?"
    "Can we cook on a typewriter?"
    "What will happen if I prick this balloon with a pin?"
    "What will happen if I polish black shoes with white polish?"
    "What will happen if I light a match and touch it to this paper?"
    "If I set this mousetrap, what will happen when I put my pencil on the cheese? What will happen when the mouse nibbles the cheese?"
    "If I put this ice in a pan over this fire, what will happen to the ice? What will happen when I put this ice in the sunshine?"

12. See what shapes the child can make when given three circles, two squares, and a triangle. Have him build other wholes from parts. (Refer to Chap. 9 for form perception activities.)

13. Use pictures to help a child predict. For example, show a picture of a wrecked car (or one with a flat tire), and a car in good condition. Ask, "Which car can someone drive?" Show a picture of a tall boy and a short boy. Ask, "Which boy will be able to reach the basket more easily in a game of basketball? Why?"

14. Raise plants and animals, predicting how they will grow.

15. Select any object, then ask, "What can we do to make it different?"

16. Evaluate and encourage logical thinking by a game of checkers.

CONCEPTUALIZATION RELATED TO CREATIVITY

The projecting of a future concept provides an opportunity for TRIAL-and-ERROR experimentation. This experimentation is tempered by the influence of a total cell assembly. It is possible that through "playing with alterations" the child can gradually develop IMAGINATION. Inventing is relating data in new ways. When past and present percepts are related differently, the resulting future prediction is a *new* idea.

Some brain-damaged children have particular, inherent talents for creativeness. But in many instances, their lack of neural structuring prohibits the expression of these talents. Teaching the child a systematic approach to conceptualization may stimulate creativity by providing guidelines along which he can more easily express what he feels.

CONCEPTUALIZATION BEGINS AT HOME

The identification and relating of stimuli must *begin* at home, while the child is very young. The approach should be methodical, first making the child aware of his own body, and then teaching him to relate himself to his world in both space and time. In this way, an inherent orderliness is learned as soon as possible. Without such pacing, relationships cannot be clearly distinguished and defined.

TIMING

Parents must establish a definite schedule for the child to assist him in his first organization of time. This translates time into a stabilized pattern within which the child can perform. The tempo of the home should be unhurried and consistent, with regular hours for getting up, meals, home responsibilities, school and play activities, and bedtime. After a schedule is established, the child will adhere to it with great acceptance and dependence, and the entire household will benefit accordingly.

ORDER WITHIN TIMING

Once a daily schedule is "enforced," the next step at home is to teach that order, within the schedule, is also expected. This order is a spatial and temporal orientation. For example, *when* the child gets up, he then puts away his night clothes, gets dressed, makes the bed, brushes his teeth, washes his hands and face, and straightens up his room. The furnishings in the child's own room should reflect the order expected of him:

> a full-length mirror so that the child can monitor his appearance;
> a dresser with drawers where each item has its own place;
> a closet with hooks and hangers for clothes, and a rack for shoes;
> a bulletin board where he can neatly tack up pictures;
> a table or cabinet for collections;
> a bed of his own;
> a chair, the correct size;
> a large blackboard for practicing drawing and writing; and
> when he is ready, a desk of his own.

Recommend a game of "pick up" each morning, to train the child to differentiate and to make decisions as he straightens his room.

At first, tasks for "order within timing" may be slow, clumsy, and "out of order." But the order can be accomplished eventually, with *great patience* and varied teaching techniques. For example, even at mealtime there is orderliness:

"Stay seated while you eat."
"Do only your share of talking."
"You must ask to be excused."
"You are to eat with good manners."

Parents should orient the child to his home and his responsible place in the family by designating tasks to him, such as dusting, sweeping, washing or drying dishes, and raking. These simple tasks make the child's "extra" time satisfying, rather than jumbled, unstructured, and confusing. Brain-damaged children must be taught *how* to carry out their responsibilities in order to develop good work habits. Learning *how* to perform the responsibility will carry over to *how well* the child performs his next responsible task. It is logical that the child who learns the meaning of responsibility at home will be many steps ahead when he moves into school where it is necessary for him to be responsible in order to learn academic lessons. As learning is achieved, the amount of time the child sticks to the task should be gradually lengthened.

Help with the organization of a job by directing: "Pick up the pan," "Wipe it all over until it is dry," "Put it away here."

Carefully evaluate how many types of responsible tasks a child can learn to perform in a number of days. Do not confuse him with too many tasks at once. It is more important for him to carry through well in a limited number of tasks than to halfheartedly perform in more.

While neatness and order have been stressed, this does not mean the brain-damaged child should never have time for informal fun. However, keep in mind that informal fun should be a "planned freedom," for even the relaxed moments may need structuring. Playing in the rain, or making mud pies are essential to the child's experiences. But he probably will need to be "taught" how to enjoy himself within these experiences.

Distinguish between having a room neat and clean because it never was cluttered up in the first place, and having a room straightened *after* it has been cluttered. Neatness should never be substituted for experimentation; it should be the result of a straightening up *after* experimentation. Both the process of experimenting *and* the process of returning an environment to an orderly state are important.

chapter 8

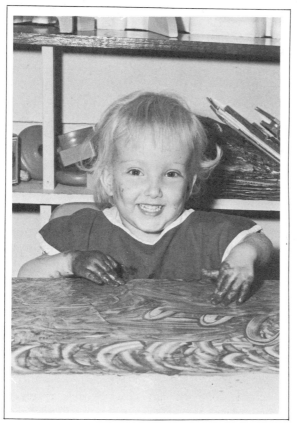

Arm and Hand Coordination

During early motor learning there is differentiation of more specific control of muscle groups out of global general movement. In the brain damaged, the differentiation is incomplete or partial, as seen particularly in shoulder-arm-hand-finger control. Consultations with physical and occupational therapists may clarify deficiencies and help in the planning of habilitation programs. Manipulation activities, such as reaching, grasping, picking-up, or releasing are very basic to learning and should be a part of the child's everyday life. Properly planned, they offer satisfaction and fun.

Consider all factors during arm and hand coordination activities. Can the child visually monitor his work and deal with spatial and temporal relationships? For example: Can he *continually see* what he is sawing? Can he relate one wire to another well enough to make flowers out of pipe cleaners? Can he sequence the complexities of tying a bow? Evaluate whether a technique is best used for only one arm, or as a bimanual activity, and whether it can encourage arm function on both sides of the midline.

STEP I—LARGE MOVEMENTS FOR ARM-HAND MANIPULATION

1. Teach the children to use GESTURES to illustrate action in songs, poems, and stories. For instance, have them move one

arm over another in "The Bear Went Over the Mountain," or in "Jack, Jump Over the Candlestick."

2. Provide a sturdy WORKBENCH at school and at home. Use a strong vise, the manipulation of which is a good exercise. Use good and sharp tools, if the child's coordination will allow. The safety of workbenches depends upon how well the children have been taught and helped to use tools properly. Teach *how to use* as well as *how to care for* the tools, so that they will stay in good repair.

   Pounding does not need to be limited to working with wood. Remove the ends from a tin can, then have the child pound the sides of the can together until it is flat. If sawing is difficult, saw wood fiber-board products, such as acoustical tile.

3. Engage the children in such activities as:
   riding an "Irish Mail" truck;
   rowing a boat one arm at a time, and then bimanually;
   using a chinning bar;
   swimming, and then practicing the same strokes out of the water;
   washing the floor or wall;
   climbing on a jungle gym;
   climbing ropes;
   pushing and pulling a wheelbarrow, or a weighted buggy;
   raking;
   sweeping;
   playing basketball (A low basketball hoop provides hours of
       satisfaction, even for a child in a wheelchair);
   jumping rope;
   doing push-ups;
   punching a punching-bag;
   rolling a car window up and down;
   turning spigots on and off;
   turning a bicycle upside down, then turning the pedals with
       hand and arm movements;
   cutting a big corrugated box apart with a serrated steak knife;
   stirring;
   opening cans and bottles;
   dishing out ice cream;
   kneading bread and cookie dough;
   washing and drying dishes.

STEP II–SPECIFIC MOVEMENTS FOR
ARM-HAND ACTIVITIES

1. Put together and take apart big plastic POP BEADS.

2. Do FINGER PAINTING. (Keep the hand as a fist to encourage wrist and arm movements.)

3. Use PASTELS (similar to chalk) on wet or dry paper. Wet the paper with water or liquid starch, and blend the colors with the fingers and hands.

4. Use ELECTRIC SCISSORS if regular scissors cannot be manipulated yet. (Some children like to hold the vibrating scissors against themselves.)

5. Wind PIPE CLEANERS (encouraging a circular movement) around pencils to make centers for paper flowers. Reinforce concept formation by verbalizing "across," "next," and "around." Wrap *heavy twine* (later varnished) around a can to make a pencil holder. Wrap *string* around a large stick, preparing the string for kite-flying. Wind a *clay* "snake" around a can. Wind *yarn* around a cottage cheese carton to make an Easter or May basket. Slit the carton from top to bottom every two inches so that the yarn winds in and out.

6. Make MUD PIES. Be sure the child has the satisfaction of seeing these when they are dry.

7. Provide a BOLT BOARD, putting numerous sizes of bolts through a board about fifteen inches long, so that the child can manipulate the nuts on and off the bolts.

8. Have the child hold onto a big stick with both hands, and then move the stick up and down or back and forth so that he "feels" BOTH ARMS MOVING TOGETHER.

9. Enjoy FINGER PLAYS.

10. CLAP in time to music.

11. Practice a TWISTING WRIST MOVEMENT by transferring a small, heavy ball or block from one hand to another. Let the object fall from one palm to the other. A jester (rotating head) that plays a tune when a stick is twirled is an excellent incentive for practicing wrist and hand movements.

FIGURE 8-1

12. TEAR PAPER into pieces, then use the pieces for some project. (Refer to Chap. 9.) Also tear out definite forms. (The number concept of one-half and two can be introduced here, as the child tears one paper in two.)

13. SQUEEZE NEWSPAPERS (paper napkins are easier) into balls for stuffing paper-sack puppets. Also play with the paper balls by throwing them into a waste basket located a challenging distance away.

14. Outline a large Christmas tree on a piece of cardboard. Then cut out five-inch squares of green tissue paper, crumple them, and paste them within the outline. Decorate the tree with colored bits of paper. (See Fig. 8-2, p. 101.)

15. Use PAPER MACHE, for making eggs for an Easter decoration.

16. STUFF stiff pieces of cardboard into envelopes. The more exactly the piece fits the envelope, the harder the task. This is also good for form perception and size consideration: "Is the cardboard larger than the envelope?" Stuffing envelopes may also motivate children to fold paper.

17. Precede BASKET WEAVING by driving large nails into a

FIGURE 8-2. A Christmas tree of squeezed paper. (Refer to p. 100.)

sturdy board so that colored string can be wound around the nails in many ways.

18. Introduce CHALKBOARD exercises (as recommended in *The Slow Learner In The Classroom*), easel painting, and free-hand drawings using crayons on newsprint.

19. Mark on a CLAY TABLET with a blunt, stiff instrument. The stiffer the clay, the harder the task. *Pressing* the clay out on the tablet (as a cookie sheet) is also a good exercise.

20. MANIPULATE HARDWARE including latches, door knobs, locks, etc., mounted on a board about four feet high and six feet long. Even a window to open and close can be built into the manipulation board. If the manipulation board, itself, can be raised and lowered, it will serve students of all heights.

21. SCREW JAR LIDS on and off. Vary the size of the jars to reinforce the concepts of "smaller" and "larger."

22. Pick up objects with TWEEZERS. Start with big tongs, and as the hand strengthens, decrease the size of the tongs and of the objects to be grasped.

23. Use HAND PUPPETS, perhaps made from paper maché. Paper finger puppets are made by attaching a one-inch circle,

with a face drawn on it, to a small paper ring that fits the top of each finger. If the child has great difficulty in moving his fingers separately, make a paper circle about three and three-quarters inches in diameter and draw a face on it. Attach this to a strip of paper about ten inches long and one and one-quarter inch wide. This larger ring fits around four fingers at once.

24. From ALUMINUM FOIL, *mold* animals and other objects such as balls, stars, triangles, or Christmas tree decorations made by wrapping red or green ribbon in and out of a squeezed foil wreath. Mold aluminum foil over a concave section of an egg carton to produce a silver bell. Use a bead for the clapper.

25. PICK UP FLAT OBJECTS: saucers turned over, coins, poker chips, buttons, and paper snips.

26. SHELL CORN to feed the birds.

27. PINCH CLOTHES PINS on and off a can top.

28. Use RUBBER PUZZLES, as they offer resistance when the pieces are put into place.

29. POKE SOAP BUBBLES AND BALLOONS. Use general arm-slapping movements, or the more refined hand movement of poking with a specific finger.

30. WRING OUT A WASH CLOTH OR SQUEEZE A SPONGE while washing dishes, taking a bath, or washing the floor and woodwork.

31. Punch holes with a PAPER PUNCH, gradually increasing the weight of the paper to increase the hand strength.

32. Manipulate CLAY. Keep a big formica-covered board for clay work, so that desk tops will not be soiled. Some clay types (in order of increasing resistance to kneading) are:

> putty (sometimes called a glazing compound, and a little sticky at first);
> Pla-Doh;
> paper maché and Shreddi-Mix;
> bread dough (offering excellent resiliency to squeezing);
> green floral clay;
> plastic clay;
> pottery clay (which hardens easily, but gives the child a permanent possession which can be glazed and baked);
> regular modeling clay.

A *non-edible* clay makes excellent Christmas tree decorations:

Mix together 4 cups flour, 1 cup salt, and 1 1/2 cups water. Knead 5 minutes, then roll clay flat with a rolling pin. Use cookie cutters to make numerous shapes. Bake 1 hour in a 350-degree oven. Spray the object with plastic to keep the salt from working out. Do not double or halve recipe.

Another recipe, containing alum, is recommended for children who tend to eat clay: Mix together 1 cup flour, 1 cup salt, 1 teaspoon alum, water, and food coloring.

33. Cut with a KNIFE AND FORK for an excellent, useful, daily bimanual activity. Provide a steak knife with small serrations along one edge. The knife cuts easily and yet is not dangerous to manipulate. Start the child cutting soft materials, such as clay, and pancakes at home. Later, expect him to cut up his own meat and solid foods.

34. Practice THROWING AND CATCHING. Begin by having the child catch a punching bag (suspended from the ceiling) as it swings toward him. Then use a bean bag which may be easier to catch than a ball. Proceed to a large-size soft ball which the child can handle easily. Also use a ball about eight inches in diameter which is knit or crocheted from wool and stuffed with nylon stockings.

35. CARRY OBJECTS which are heavy, or which are difficult to balance. For instance, carry one glass of water with two hands, one glass of water in one hand, or one glass of water in each hand.

36. STRING OBJECTS, such as spools, beads, or buttons. (Add an order to the stringing pattern to aid counting and sequencing.) String macaroni dyed with food coloring dissolved in rubbing alcohol.

STEP III—ADVANCED ARM-HAND ACTIVITIES

1. FOLD PAPER, even though it may be very difficult at first. Just being able to get the edges of the paper lined up evenly, and creased requires *eye-hand coordination*, *hand strength*, and accurate awareness of spatial relationships. Verbal directions assume an awareness of directionality:

a. Obtain check books with several checks on each page. These checks should be separated from one another by small perforations. Paper with *perforated* guidelines is easier to fold than plain paper. Other perforated paper can be prepared by "sewing" with an unthreaded sewing machine.

b. Fold a large sheet of newsprint into a series of folds parallel to one another; fold the paper in two, then fold in two again. Hold the paper with the non-dominant hand and crease with the dominant. Then unfold the paper and trace the folds with a thick pencil or crayon to reinforce the horizontal or vertical aspect of the line. Use the paper for writing lessons and art projects. Fold pretend mail for classroom delivery.

c. Proceed to fold the paper lengthwise and crosswise so that there are both horizontal and perpendicular lines. *Squares*, which can be cut out or outlined for numerous uses, result. For instance, practice diagonal lines by drawing from one corner of the square to another.

d. Refer to several books on paper folding for detailed directions on how to fold paper to make a hat, a boat, or more complicated objects. Use wallpaper samples and origami papers to make the objects attractive. With much practice, the art of paper folding allows a handicapped child to be creative.

2. Begin LACING with a masonite circle, about ten inches in diameter, with three-quarter inch holes punched around the edge. Use a long shoe lace to go in and out of the holes. Later, proceed to lacing yarn around a paper plate; then use commercial sewing cards:

FIGURE 8-3

3. Teach the child to BUTTON, ZIP, AND TIE by having him practice in front of himself, rather than on clothes he is actually wearing, because: a. some handicapped children tire very quickly if they must hold themselves in an awkward position for any length of time, b. the child can experience the "feel" of the task before he attempts it in the more awkward position, and c. those children depending upon *visual clues* will learn more rapidly by *seeing* the task.

Introduce buttoning with a quilted nylon house-coat, hanging so that the child can sit comfortably while he practices. The quilted nylon allows buttons to be moved through button holes with minimum effort.

Emphasize zipping as a bimanual task, since the bottom of the zipper must be held with the non-dominant hand. A child who zips up and snaps his own jeans has accomplished a big step, and gets *daily* well-motivated practice with this hand manipulation.

To aid motivation, vary the places where the child ties. Use a big shoe, a post with a big shoestring around it, or an attractive tying board:

FIGURE 8-4

Use color clueing to differentiate between the two laces being tied together: "Wrap the red lace around the white one."

Be sure all persons teaching the child use a consistent approach, since "what comes next" and "what goes where" should always be the same. For example, when beginning to tie, in-

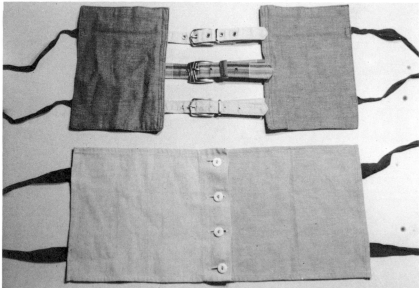

FIGURE 8-5. Finger manipulation exercises. (Refer to p. 107.)

struct the child to lay the laces in an "X" pattern with one over the other. Then, "The top lace goes *under* the other one, and back up toward you. Now pull the laces tight."

Pictured in Fig. 8-5, p. 106 are wide bands to be tied around a child when he manipulates buttons, zippers, and buckles. Also pictured are interesting items to motivate buttoning practice.

4. Use PIPE CLEANERS for making decorations and figures such as letters and numbers. Pliers may be necessary to hold the wires firmly.

5. SEW on buttons.

6. Draw around the inside and outside of a STENCIL, holding the stencil with the non-dominant hand.

7. WRAP pretty packages.

8. "Pour" SHELLED CORN from one container to another. The smaller the container, the harder the task.

9. Build with TINKERTOYS, and, later, erector sets.

10. HOOK rugs and hangings.

11. Teach TYPING to advanced students. Even the "hunt and peck" system provides communication for children unable to write. Consider a primary typewriter if the child has difficulty *seeing* the letters he is typing. Consider an electric typewriter for children with good hand control but little strength.

chapter 9

Cutting with Scissors

Readiness skills for cutting with scissors include hand dominance, arm-hand coordination, perseveration correction, and eye-hand coordination. Select scissors that cut well and are appropriate for the right or left hand. Keep the child motivated by good use of his creations.

STEP I—CUTTING CLAY AND COTTON

Develop the "cutting" motion of the dominant hand, and the "holding" motion of the other by cutting clay into little pieces. (Pretend these pieces are cookies, and put them into a little dish or pie pan.) Unlike paper, clay can be held in any position to be cut; at first, it does not *have* to be held at all. If necessary, the teacher's hands should manipulate the child's through the releasing and closing movements of using the scissors. For variety, cut little chunks of cotton and paste them *on* the outline, or *inside* the outline, of a "snowman." Paste pieces of the cotton on a tree branch for snow or pussy willows. Fill in the outline of a little lamb with bits of cotton.

STEP II—CUTTING PAPER SNIPS

"Snips" are bits of paper cut at random. (Pieces of paper straws can be used as snips, or for stringing.) Uses for snips include:

1. Complete pictures by using snips for tree leaves (vary the color with the seasons) or for filling in an outline. (See Fig. 9-1.)

Use an assortment of brown, black and white snips to form a cobblestone pathway.

FIGURE 9-1

2. Paste snips on plain papers to make random designs. Vary the textures and types of papers to add interest.

3. Use snips for decorations and special effects. Decorate a green construction-paper Christmas tree or a green wreath with multi-colored snips, or use white snips for "snow" against a black background.

STEP III—CUTTING ALONG A STRAIGHT LINE

Although a child can cut along a straight line with someone else holding the paper, he should begin to hold the paper in his non-dominant hand so that cutting becomes a *bimanual* process. Hold the blades of the scissors at a 90-degree angle to the paper so that the scissors actually cut and do not just slide over the paper. Visually impaired children begin to have difficulties at this step, and will need reminding to "Slow down," and to "Watch the line."

At first, expect the child to cut along a *short* line, only two inches long; then increase this length as the child improves. Use strip cutting in combination with other techniques. For example, if the child is advanced in his use of a pencil or crayon, let him draw a straight line with a ruler, and then cut along it. Or cut along a folded line. *Emphasize* the straight line to be cut by:

1. making it thicker (using crayon or magic marker);

2. making it a different color;

3. providing tactile guidelines for a seriously handicapped child by mounting two strips of cardboard on a sheet of paper and having the child cut between them; or, with increased coordination, using only one piece of cardboard.

Uses for strips:

1. Paste the ends of strips together to make *ringlets*. Surround a happy face with ringlets for hair, or use white ringlets for Santa's beard and hair. Paste white or black ringlets inside the outline of a sheep. Use green ringlets for a Christmas tree:

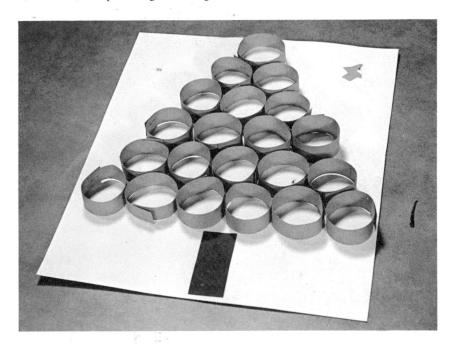

FIGURE 9-2

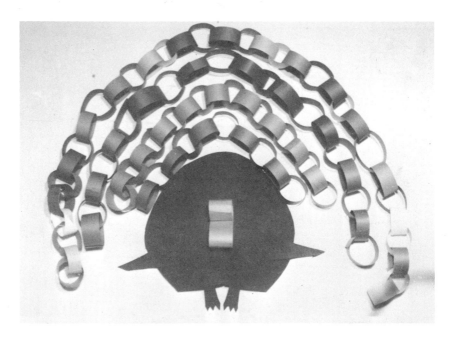

FIGURE 9-3.   For cutting motivation, create paper-chain objects. (Refer to p. 113.)

2. Loop ringlets together for *chains* for decorating rooms, and as necklaces and bracelets. Vary the colors to make the chains seasonal. Use a chain around a colored circle to make a flower, and use chains for arms and legs of large figures. Illustrated in Fig. 9-3, p. 112 are a flag and turkey formed from chains.

3. Cut strips into snips.

4. Make *springs* by folding two strips back and forth over each other to produce an accordion-like effect. Amusing animals can be formed with these:

FIGURE 9-4

5. Make *random designs* on paper.

6. Weave *paper mats* and *May baskets*.

STEP IV—CUTTING STRAIGHT LINES WITH TURNS

Straight lines with turns include geometric figures: squares, triangles, and rhomboids. Teach the child to *turn* the paper with his helping hand, and to *stop* cutting before he turns the paper. Let him begin by cutting around angles larger than 90 degrees, and proceed to sharper corners. Examples of numerous designs the student can make with his new skill are pictured:

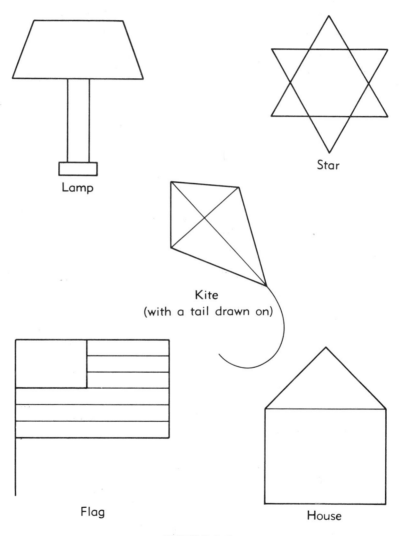

FIGURE 9-5

By folding a paper several times and then making cut-outs in the paper, lacy effects are produced. Mount these on paper of a contrasting color for place mats or greeting cards.

STEP V—CUTTING CURVED LINES AND CIRCLES

The paper must be turned continuously when cutting curved lines and circles. Have the child start by cutting short, curved lines clearly

FIGURE 9-6. Combining circles with strips and geometric forms. (Refer to p. 116.)

drawn on paper. Next, let him cut out large circles, gradually decreasing the size as he develops skill. Uses for the circles include:

1. arranging them, in descending size, on top of each other, or arranging them in ascending or descending order across a sheet of colored paper;

2. overlapping numerous green circles of the same size to make a long "caterpillar," with a face and feelers drawn on the first circle;

3. making a teepee (or cone effect) by slitting a circle to the center and then overlapping the cut edges and pasting them together;

4. designing greeting cards with circles cut from wallpaper;

5. developing forms by combining circles with strips and geometric forms. (See Fig. 9-6, p. 115.)

STEP VI—CUTTING COMBINATIONS OF SHAPES

Now cut out *combinations* of the forms with which the child has already been working, such as:

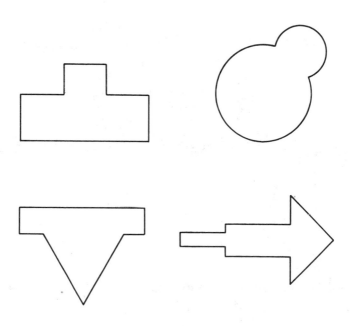

FIGURE 9-7

Gradually the complexity of the design should be increased, until the child is prepared to try simple, irregular forms found in beginning coloring books.

STEP VII–CUTTING EASY FIGURES

When cutting out a pictured object, the child may have as much trouble deciding on *which* line to cut as with the manipulation of the scissors:

FIGURE 9-8

Therefore, introduce these aids:

1. Use a definite color to *outline* the object;

2. Run the child's finger around the outline *before* he starts to cut;

3. Color the figure, so that it will be easier to recognize the *whole* form.

STEP VIII—CUTTING VARIATIONS

To provide reinforcement of hand manipulation, and advanced cutting:

1. Cut with *pinking shears* which are more difficult to manipulate than regular scissors. Use them for any of the activities recommended for regular scissors.

2. Cut materials that are heavier than paper, such as *sewing scraps* of differing weights, and *tagboard* and *heavier cardboard.* One teacher tells of asking a fifteen-year-old student to "Cut out something in this magazine." Much to the teacher's amazement, the boy selected a figure on the cover of the magazine and promptly cut it out—cutting through the *whole* magazine as he went along! This is not a recommended procedure, but it does remind a teacher to make a child's hand work a little harder by putting additional sheets of paper under the one he is cutting.

3. Cut *string and yarn:* Make random designs with the pieces, or paste them along the outline of a figure. Weave string into mesh vegetable sacks which can be hung up in trees to furnish material for the birds at nest-building time.

4. Cut *aluminum pie pans:* Make numerous slits from the edge of the pan to the circle that forms the bottom of the pan. Cut out Christmas pictures to glue in the circle, and use the decoration for the Christmas tree.

5. Cut *crayons:* Scatter snips of crayon on a doubled sheet of wax paper, with two more pieces of waxed paper on top. Place all of this on a pile of newspapers and iron the surface of the waxed paper, from the center outward, using a moderate iron. The transparency resulting from the melted crayons within the fused sheets of waxed paper can be framed with construction paper and hung in a window.

Use ordinary manilla paper instead of waxed paper, with one sheet on each side of the crayon chips. After ironing, separate the two sheets to reveal a "modern art" design on each.

CONCERNING THE CHILD WHO WANTS TO CUT BEYOND HIS ABILITIES

What can be done about the frustrated child who wants to cut out complex forms before he is ready to control his scissors? Solve this by drawing a circle, square, or triangle *around* the complex figure. By cutting on these easy lines, the child has the satisfaction, for example, of having "cut out a doll."

chapter 10

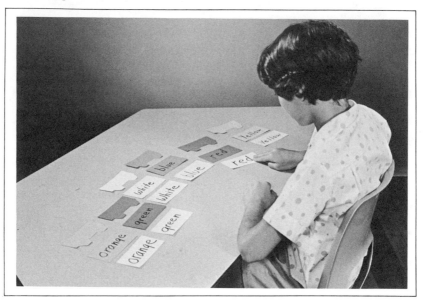

Pre-Reading

READINESS ABILITIES

Basic to pre-reading are verbal, visual, and auditory readiness abilities. Speech is not imperative, although children are generally handicapped in their approach to written language if experience with the spoken language has been limited, since oral reading unites visual and auditory stimuli. The response to auditory stimuli includes auditory memory and discrimination related to the *quality* of sound, as well as auditory discrimination related to *temporal* aspects, or sequencing. (See Chaps. 5 and 6.) The *quality* of the sound is important in differentiating a short vowel from a long one, for example. The *temporal* aspect is important as letters are put together for blendings or words, since the child must hear the temporal arrangement of the "l" coming *after* the "b" in a "bl" blend; he must also phonetically relate letters and syllables to form words, and he should relate words to form sentences read with correct emphasis and speed.

Although the perception of a form is imperative, the recognition of the form per se, and the separation of this form from its background (the figure-ground relationship), are not the only visual considerations of pre-reading lessons. Visual memory and visual sequencing (the recognition of the relationship in space of objects to one another) are also important, and have been emphasized in Chap. 6. Visual and auditory memory allow a child to accumulate a basic, beginning reading vocabulary. Visual sequencing, a form of spatial discrimination, becomes important as the child sees how letters relate spatially to form a word.

The recognition of basic shapes, resulting in the recognition of letters and words, necessitates a specialized, methodical approach for some brain-damaged children, and includes steps for recognizing shapes by gross-motor, fine-motor, and visual perception. Of three basic shapes, the easiest to learn is the *circle*. It has no corners, it simply goes "around and around." The square "has corners" or "places where one must stop and turn." "It has four corners and four sides." The triangle "has three sharp corners and three sides." "You start to make a triangle the same way you start to make an Indian teepee." To avoid confusion, teach only one basic shape at a time. Then, after each is learned, they can be compared.

STEP I—GROSS-MOTOR ACTIVITIES FOR BASIC SHAPES

It is not enough for a brain-damaged child to begin to perceive shapes with only his eyes. The combined feedback from using his whole body to explore and experience a shape gives the most clues as to why the shape is distinct. It is encouraging that a child can begin his learning of basic shapes through gross-motor activities because they can be experienced by almost all children. Even uncoordinated children can be manipulated through a specific pattern.

LEARNING ABOUT A CIRCLE:

1. Have the child walk (or crawl) along a circle design (about eight or ten feet in diameter) made with colored adhesive tape on the floor. He should get the feeling of going "around, and around, and around." Have him move clockwise and counterclockwise.

2. Have two children stand and hold hands as they jump and move in a circle on the trampoline.

3. Stand behind the child, holding his arm by the wrist, in order to control both his arm and hand. Put this arm through the motions of a circle, saying "around and around." Go clockwise and counterclockwise; finally do the exercise with both arms. For motiva-

tion, have the child hold a colored streamer. Also, put the child in front of the chalkboard so that his motions make circles on the chalkboard. Afterwards, trace the chalkline with his fist or finger.

4. Draw a large continuing concentric (spiral) design on a big sheet of paper. Direct the child to "drive a car" along the circular design, using a very small toy car.

LEARNING ABOUT A SQUARE:

1. Have the child walk (or crawl) along a square design (about ten feet square) made with colored adhesive tape on the floor. The child learns a "corner" is a "turn," and his whole body will turn. As he learns *what* a corner is, he can count from 1 to 4 as he turns the corners. For motivation, the child can pretend that he is a soldier, and that each corner is a "Halt," "Right Face," "Go."

2. Reinforce corners by a top-hat design taped on the floor. Make the design so that each turn is about twenty-seven inches from the next turn.

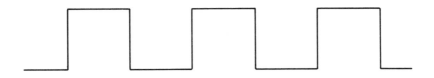

FIGURE 10-1

For motivation, the corners can be "gas stations," or houses of friends, where the child must stop for a moment.

3. Have the child drive his toy racer around a "race track" created by a continuing concentric square on a large sheet of paper.

4. Stand behind the child, holding his arm by the wrist. Put his arm through the motions of a square, emphasizing the "stop," "turn," and "start" at the corners. Eventually, directions are "line," "corner," "line," "corner." Do this design with each arm, then with both arms together, going in the same direction. Do the same exercise in front of a big chalkboard, so that a square

is drawn. Trace the design with the child's fist or hand. If necessary, emphasize corners with an "x" or colored mark. Use a
paintbrush or crayon to draw on a big sheet of paper clamped
to an easel.

5. Add an *auditory* clue to the recognition of a corner. Ring a bell
or beat a drum when the child should turn.

6. Structure the beginning concept of form by making a *starting
point* on the chalkboard or paper, using a big dot or an "x."
Then give verbal instructions regarding the directions of the
lines. For a square, use terms such as "horizontal," "across,"
"vertical," "down," "up," "right," and "left." The beginning dot
is placed at the *bottom, left;* the "line" of lined paper also provides this same starting point, only the indication is less em-

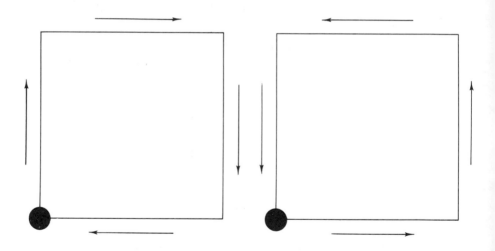

FIGURE 10-2

phatic. This orientation is important, as emphasized again in the
pre-writing chapter, since brain-damaged children need a starting point in space, as well as left-to-right orientation. By this
technique the child receives concrete, accurate directions that
he can apply to other teaching situations. He also draws the
form, without segmentation, in one continuous series of movements.

LEARNING ABOUT A TRIANGLE:

1. Design a triangle, five feet on each side, with colored adhesive tape on the floor. As the child moves along this design, he should note the corners are "much sharper" (or "faster turns") than those on the square. (When preparing such a design on the floor, be sure the sides are not so long that the child loses the concept of the *total* form.)

2. Reinforce the concept of sharp corners by taping a mountain design on the floor, along which the child can walk, or crawl, and still get the idea of acute angles:

FIGURE 10-3

3. Stand behind the child and put his arms through movements outlining the shape of a triangle, as recommended for the circle and square. Reinforce the concept with the chalkboard, in painting or coloring activities recommended for the square and circle. *Be sure you put the child through these activities, even if he is not capable of moving his limbs the way he wants to himself.*

4. At the chalkboard, make an "x" or a dot for a starting point at the *bottom*, *left* corner of the triangle, then have the child make the triangle according to the teacher's verbal directions. New words must be learned, such as: "oblique," "diagonal," and "slanted." Discourage segmentation of the form, and show the child how to draw the triangle in a continuous movement. Go in both directions from the beginning point. (Do not move on to the next step in pre-reading until the student grasps the idea of a corner, and the concept that a circle, square, and triangle are different.

STEP II–FINE-MOTOR ACTIVITIES FOR BASIC SHAPES

1. Use a *simple wooden puzzle* for beginning form perception. The child can *see* and *feel* the shapes.[1] Note that a child can feel better if his arms and hands are relaxed. If there is maximum muscle tonus, then there is minimum kinesthetic feedback for discerning contrast. Therefore, consider physical therapy techniques for relaxation and better tactual recognition of figure-ground relationships.

2. Cut a set of *basic shapes* out of colored poster board. Include: 3 red equilateral triangles, 9 inches per side; 3 red equilateral triangles, 6½ inches per side; 3 red squares, 9 inches square; 3 red squares, 6 inches square; 3 red circles, 9 inches in diameter; and 3 red circles, 6½ inches in diameter. Teach the child to match the shapes that are alike. He should *say* the name of the shape as he places it in the correct place, learning by seeing, feeling, and hearing. If he is confused by *two* sizes of the same shape, start with only *one* size of each shape. Likewise, if it is too confusing for the child to deal with *three* shapes at the same time, start teaching with only the circle shapes, and gradually add the square and triangle.

    As the child learns, add to the original Poster-Board Set of Basic Shapes by duplicating the red set in green, yellow, and blue (or black, white, etc.).

    Make the total exercise more complicated by presenting forms of *varying* colors to match, by shape. Vary the size of the shapes for an even more complicated exercise, initiating the child's learning of the concepts of "big" and "little." Instruct, "Get the big, red circle." As the number of descriptive adjectives added to the shape is increased, the task becomes harder. The child may recognize "the big circle," and "the red circle," but when the descriptions are put together, the selection becomes more complicated.

3. Use the *flannelboard* in combination with the Poster-Board Set of Basic Shapes. Place a large flannelboard in front of the room. *Say* the name of the basic shape as the child places it in the correct row. There is learning reinforcement by *seeing, feeling,*

---

[1]Recommended is a puzzle by Childcare Co., Loveland, Colorado. This first puzzle includes a circle, square, and triangle. A more advanced puzzle provides six shapes.

and *hearing*. (It is more effective for the *children* to use the flannelboard than for the teacher herself to place the shapes on it while the children say the correct name. The participation of the children is a motivating factor for them.) Put a piece of colored yarn along the center of each row of like shapes on the flannelboard. This line of yarn helps the child to visually associate like shapes.

4. Use *templates*, made from a durable substance such as masonite. These allow the child to *feel* and *see* a basic form. The templates are also recommended in the pre-writing section. Vary the sizes as the child learns. However, several beginning basic sizes and shapes are recommended:

Circle	*Square*	*Triangle*
Outside diameter: 7½ in.	Outside edge: 7 in.	Outside edge: 8 in.
Cut-out diameter: 4½ in.	Cut-out edge: 4 in.	Cut-out edge: 4½ in.

Smaller circle

Outside diameter: 5½ in.
Cut-out diameter: 2½ in.

Due to the hand coordination required, the *inside*, cut-out edge of the template is easier to trace around than the *outside* edge. In the inside, direction is guided and confined.

5. *Use materials for teaching blind children.* In some booklets, basic shapes are made of a raised, fuzzy substance set against a particularly smooth background, so that the child can easily differentiate the form he is learning. Have the child close his eyes and verbally identify the shape.

6. Prepare *kinesthetic* materials. Use sandpaper, felt, or rough-textured materials to make outlines of the basic shapes to identify, as in (5). Prepare a *loose-leafed scrapbook* with a basic shape on each page. Put the pages in different order occasionally, to avoid the identification of shapes by memory of their order in the book. Use stencils of shapes to be compared. Place these over sandpaper for the child to feel.

7. Draw *outlines of basic shapes* on a large piece of paper, and have the student place the proper shape within each outline. The Poster-Board Set of Basic Shapes can be used. Require verbal identification of each shape.

8. Look for basic shapes in pictures or in the environment. Prepare a scrapbook of pictures including a clock "with a circle

face," "a square house," etc. Take the child on tours inside and outside the classroom to see what shapes he can find.

9. Use many *printed exercises* where shapes similar to the first are to be underlined, "x'd" or circled.

10. Test visual perception (form constancy) against varying backgrounds:

    a. Place the basic form against such background textures as silk, wool, flannel, felt, and linen. Use different colors for both the shapes and backgrounds. Use smooth and rough surfaces, so that the child *feels* and *sees* the shape in contrast to the surface. Have him pick up the form so that he can *experience* it as apart from the background.

    b. Place the basic form against paper surfaces which gradually become more distracting as a background. Again, let the child feel, see, and experience the relationship of the form and its background:

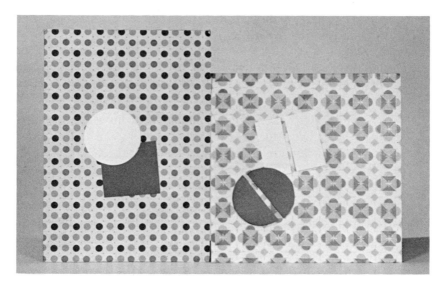

FIGURE 10-4

STEP III—LEARNING VARIED SHAPES

When the child can easily recognize a circle, triangle, and square, investigate additional shapes. Match and compare these in the same ways recommended in STEP II, including the wooden puzzle that expands the number of shapes to six. Add these additional shapes to the Poster-Board Set, so that the child can arrange like shapes in horizontal or vertical rows, or pile them neatly on top of one another.

1. Teach recognition of forms by having the child *feel blocks* which have been put into a cloth bag, as a pillowcase. Use the wooden shapes from the previously inspected puzzles. Have the child reach into the bag, take one shape, and feel it without looking at it. Then he can point to the place on the puzzle where the piece fits. Also, put some of the shapes or objects *behind* the child, having him identify them, one by one.

    Note: The fact that the objects are *behind* the child may make the task more complicated, depending upon the child's knowledge of his own body image. Some children get lost when considering "behind" themselves. If the child has trouble here, reinforce his learning by exercises to teach body image and laterality. (See Chap. 5.) Blindfold the child and put cubes or spheres of varying sizes on a table. Have him arrange them according to size *or* shape. Eventually, he should arrange them by size *and* shape.

2. Use a *dice game* to challenge the student's form perception. Take a plain block of wood 1½ to 2 inches square; on the sides of it paint the shapes the child is learning. Use six or less different shapes. Each child is given his own "man" to move. On a large piece of cardboard, prepare a "trail" of sections on which the matching six shapes are painted. The child rolls the block to see where he will move along the trail. The first child to get over the trail wins!

3. *Mold Pla-Doh or clay* for copying the shape of a form. A child with hand coordination too poor to draw or trace a square gains satisfaction from rolling clay into a long strip, and then shaping it into a square. By this method, teachers have discovered that some children *do* have insight into a shape, even though they cannot draw it or verbalize it.

4. Provide *rubber puzzles* with numerous shapes cut out. In addition to the use for form perception, the manipulative benefit to hand muscles is excellent. Rubber puzzles vary in resistance, and should be presented for the child to manipulate according to *increasing* resistance.

5. Prepare *lotto and bingo* games.

6. Provide sets of *seasonal cards* with decorative shapes which can be sorted:

FIGURE 10-5

7. Make exercises, where *similar shapes* are to be circled, "x'd," or underlined, more complicated by filling in parts of the forms with color:

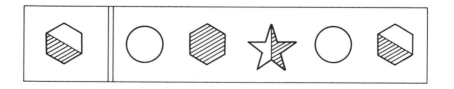

FIGURE 10-6

STEP IV—RECOGNIZING COMBINATIONS OF SHAPES, AND MANIPULATING PATTERNS

Begin exercises challenging the child's more exact discernment of forms.

1. Present *combinations* of the forms already used, such as:

FIGURE 10-7

If the forms are put on cards, request the child to place the card beside or on top of the like form. Even the size of the forms can be varied for careful scrutiny:

 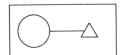 

FIGURE 10-8

2. Prepare a *Form-Manipulation Poster-Board Set* which can be enlarged to make designs more complex. The set offers shapes which can be manipulated to *make* and *rearrange* patterns: 2 red and 2 blue triangles, 6½ in. along each side; 4 red and 4 blue circles, 2½ in. in diameter; 2 red and 2 blue squares, 4 in. along each side.

FIGURE 10-9

Note that in the photograph, the student's design is a mirror-image of the teacher's design. This should not be so, unless requested. Always refer to the "right," "left," "top," or "bottom" of the pattern. If you are facing the child while you work, be certain you refer to the child's right and left, not your own. It is important to his future learning *that the student become oriented to patterns in relation to himself.*

2a. Reinforce the learning of patterns by having the child draw, on paper or on the chalkboard, the same design he has just made with the Form-Manipulation Poster-Board Set. Gradually, the child should be able to copy similar designs, *from* paper, *onto* paper because of his previous experiences with the actual manipulative materials.

3. Use *form boards* for the development of pattern manipulation. (Refer to the Appendix for detailed directions.)

   One type of form board has pegs extending up from a solid surface. Place large stringing beads on the pegs to make different patterns, according to color and size. Start with very simple patterns, and increase their complexity as the child learns. This type of form board is particularly good for children having difficulty releasing objects from their hands, as the pegs hold the object in place until release occurs.

4. Provide *parquetry blocks* of all sizes for pattern development. Have the child place his blocks on top of a design drawn on paper. Start with the simplest pattern, using only two blocks. Finally, teach the child to reconstruct a design, copying first the teacher's design made from the blocks, and then a representation of the block design on paper.

5. Manipulate *pipe cleaners, tongue blades, sticks of clay, toothpicks,* and *paste sticks.* Make stick designs and request the student to copy them. Next, *draw* a stick design and ask the student to make a similar one with his pipe cleaners, etc.

6. Construct *a house from flannel or poster board,* consisting of: 2 squares, each 6 in. square; 2 triangles, each 6 in. on a side; 8 small squares, each 1½ in. square, in a contrasting color to the big squares; and 4 small rectangles, each 1 in. by 2 in., in a contrasting color to the big squares. Slice diagonally across two of the rectangles to be used for chimneys. By copying the patterns of the teacher, the child creates a house:

FIGURE 10-10

7. Strengthen form perception with *commercial lotto games*. Do not confuse the simple *matching* games with those of association. Only the matching forms should be used at this level, as association deals with form perception *and* relationships according to use.

8. Prepare *Imitation of Movement Cards* illustrating movements of the arms and legs. Make three cards of each design for the child to match. For reinforcement, have the child act out the movements pictured. The first cards should depict figures with the arms held straight. (See Fig. 10-11, p. 134.) A second set should depict figures with elbows bent. (See Fig. 10-12, p. 134.)

9. Provide silhouettes of simple forms or actions. Can the child match these with the more detailed pictures?

10. Prepare *numerous cards with varied patterns*. At first, the child should be asked to sort only two different patterns of the same type. Then, with learning, add variations of the same pattern.

11. Sort sets of *cards of line drawings* of increasing complexity, approaching the forms of manuscript letters. (See Fig. 10-13, p. 135.)

12. *Coordinate visual perception with hand control* by providing exercises involving completion of a second figure to look like the first. If the child cannot hold a pencil well, he may be able to *tell* you how to finish the design. Reinforce this *completion of forms*, or *closure*, by providing large pieces of paper on

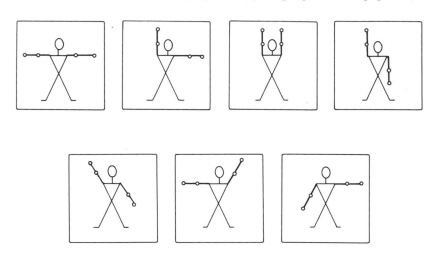

FIGURE 10-11. Imitation of movement with straight arms. (Refer to p. 133.)

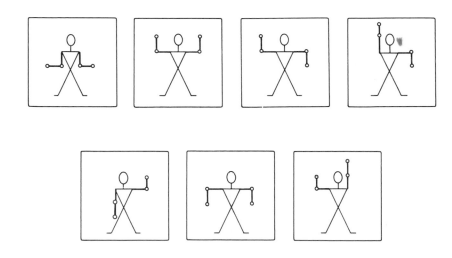

FIGURE 10-12. Imitation of movement with bent elbows. (Refer to p. 133.)

FIGURE 10-13. Compare line drawings for form discrimination. (Refer to p. 133.)

which are pasted a half, or larger portion, of a figure familiar to the child. Use, for example, a half of a house or a half of a big face. Can the child begin to represent the total figure by drawing the outlines to complete it on the plain paper? Also reinforce closure by using puzzles of geometric forms which are cut into two and then more pieces.

STEP V—RECOGNIZING MANUSCRIPT LETTERS

At this step, the child sorts the letters of the alphabet by their distinct *forms*, preceding identification by the name or sound of the letter.

1. Prepare a *card set of the alphabet*, with three cards of each letter. Have the child sort only two or three letters that are obviously different in form, as "O," "T," and "M." Add additional letters as learning permits. Reinforce this technique by sorting anagrams. Be sure the letters are clear and large enough for the child to see. Add a tactual approach by sorting plastic, wooden, and textured letters.

2. Provide printed exercises to circle, "x," or underline a letter matching the first one presented.

STEP VI–BEGINNING WORD RECOGNITION
BY VISUAL AND AUDITORY MEMORY

At this time it is not necessary for the child to learn that letters have specific names, but he should know that there are symbols (the letters) to be recognized as a *whole grouping*. Note that the whole word involves a *spatial sequencing* of letters in a *left-to-right* order. Therefore, if the child is having difficulty with direction, "order," including "beginning" and "end," will not be meaningful, and the child may:

    a.   show reversals in the order of written work: d-o-g will be written g-o-d or o-d-g;

    b.   show confusion between words being read: "top" as "pot," or "rat" as "tar."

TECHNIQUES TO BEGIN WORD RECOGNITION BY SIGHT

1.   Since proper names, initially his name and those of his friends, are of particular interest to the child, provide a *first-name identification game* by putting each child's name at the front of his desk. Mix up the names and instruct the children to put them on the correct desks.

2.   Cut appealing *forms from different colors* of construction paper. Then prepare flash cards, from the matching construction paper, with printed names of the identifying color of each. Teach the child to match the forms with the correct flash card. Next, prepare flash cards with the names of the colors on white construction paper. Can the child match these white cards to the colored cards? Finally, teach the child how to match the white cards to the object of the correct color. (See photograph at the beginning of this chapter.)

3.   *Identify objects and places*, such as "door," "window," "books," "chair," and "wall" with word cards. Ask the child's parents to make word cards identifying things at home. For example, the child's drawers can be labeled "socks," "shirts," "pants," and "pajamas." This promotes neatness as well as word recognition!

4.   Present flash cards with the same words as those found in the child's preprimer. Make three or more cards of each word, and have the child sort these into like rows.

5. Provide *lotto-bingo* games for word matching. Select a number of familiar preprimer words to put on flash cards. Then make a large bingo card for each player by listing a selection of some of the words on the cards. Use the flash cards to cover the words, and proceed as in a regular lotto game.

   Note: There are two learning stages. At first the teacher instructs, "Find the word on your card that *looks like* this word," (visual identification). Later, when the children are identifying words *by what they say* (auditory-visual identification) the teacher asks, "Who has the word that *says* 'dog'?"

6. Use *printed exercises* where the student is required to circle, "x," or underline identical words. A printed exercise is more difficult when the student is required to pick out the word *unlike* the other words.

7. Reinforce *visual memory recognition* (internal visualization) of a word by placing a word card in front of the child. Then take the card away and present two cards, one of which is the one just studied. Ask the child to select the one he has studied. The more *dissimilar* the form of the two words, such as "boy" and "Jane," the easier the step. As learning proceeds, the two words can be more similar in total form, such as "boy" and "toy."

   Increase the difficulty of this exercise by adding additional cards to be recognized. For example, have the child study *two* cards. Take them away and then have him choose these two words from three cards presented.

8. Play "Password." Each day put a new "password" on the door of the room, which the child identifies as he enters and leaves.

9. Purchase or prepare many pictures of objects to be matched with the correct word. Also purchase a set of rubber stamps, illustrating a variety of objects and words, for "printing" after they are pressed against an inked pad. The child stamps the object on paper and then prints the word identification below.

TECHNIQUES FOR WORD RECOGNITION BY SIGHT AND SOUND

If the child can speak, as he manipulates and matches words, he will begin to say what the word says. Reinforcing lessons aid in the verbal identification:

1. Use *flash cards* to give the child the opportunity to *see* a word and to *say* it. Supplement this learning with classroom activities that help the words to be meaningful. Action words such as "run" and "jump" should actually be performed by the child, associating the action with saying or seeing.

2. *List words* at the front of the room. As the teacher says a word, the student points to the correct one.

3. Put only *one word-card* up for observation. Then say several words, one of which must be selected by the child to match.

STEP VII—BEGINNING READING BY SIGHT-MEMORY

Teach the child to read *from the left to the right*. In addition to the student's everyday experiences, several left-to-right learning activities are suggested:

1. Begin at the left end of the lines pictured, naming each picture of the animal in proper order. Many strips similar to this one can be made in a scrapbook by the teacher:

FIGURE 10-14

The child reads: "Fish, cow, rat, cat, horse." Geometric shapes and colors can be used in the same type of exercise.

2. Substitute *pictures for words* in simple stories. The teacher reads the words, and the child "reads" the pictures. Such stories are often found in children's magazines.

3. Use the *form board* to supplement left-to-right movement. Have the child place objects (colors, numbers, letters, or words) in

the sections, going from left to right. When the form board is full, the child reads what he has put into the sections.

Begin reading in a *preprimer*, but do not require that the child re-read the same book. Order preprimers from several different publishers to encourage variety rather than drill. Also, make preprimers of your own, telling simple stories of particular interest to the children. Experience stories can be included here, and stories made up by the children are usually read with great enthusiasm. Parents can also help the child to develop simple sentences at home. Base stories on experiences, such as field trips, or on letters received and written. One classroom had just been given a goldfish in a bowl. They voted on a name for the fish, and they took turns feeding it. They dictated and later read:

> Today we have a new fish.
> The fish is gold.
> We like our new fish.
> The name of our fish is Bambi.
> Steve feeds the fish.
> Our fish likes the food.
> Our fish likes to swim.

Once a child has sight-read from a set of preprimers, it is assumed that his sight vocabulary will be from 50 to 70 words or more. As the child reads these "crutches" may be helpful:

1. Cover all words except the one being read, avoiding confusion with adjoining words.

2. Cover all lines but the one being read.

3. Have the child put the first finger of his left hand at the beginning of a line and the first finger of his right hand at the end of a line, to define the immediate area in which he is to work.

4. Allow the child to follow the words by putting his finger underneath the word. The eye-hand cooperation reinforces his attention, and also helps him keep his place if he has a visual problem.

If the visual problem of the brain-damaged child is acute, it may be necessary to aid reading by making a large duplicate of the book. Then the *words* and *lines* can be *spaced further apart* to aid in spatial perception, and the *print can be larger*, allowing a larger area on which the eyes can converge. Use paper that is larger than the preprimer. Paste the picture (from the preprimer) at the top of the page. Print with a magic marker or dark crayon (for more contrast), or use a primary typewriter. Reprint the book, including: larger lettering, more space between the words and lines, color cueing, and emphasis by *underlining* or *boxing in*. Rewrite a book for some children by using *cursive* writing which will help to hold the words together.

READING WITH THE HELP OF A TAPE RECORDER

Aid and check reading progress by using a tape recorder. The teacher should record each page of the preprimer, saying the words very slowly. Then the student can *listen* to the words and *follow this verbal stimulus* with his finger and/or eyes on the printed page. Watch to see that the student follows the words correctly and turns the page at the proper time. Limit the number of pages to be read by the student's ability to keep at the task. Often, only a few pages at a time is enough for a beginning. Experiment by including a *discussion* of the *pictures* on each page in the recorded lesson. This helps to break the monotony of reading and also adds to the story's interest. Be sure to include "Turn the page."

READING WITH THE HELP OF MACHINES WHICH PROJECT AND SAY WORDS

Project a single word on a screen in front of the child. The child *sees* the word and *says* it. Some machines will even say the word for the child until he learns it himself. Or, synchronize a recorder with a projector, so that sight and sound are reinforced. By synchronization, the speed of the word projection can be controlled and increased as the child learns. This method is an excellent *impersonal* approach to word learning.

STEP VIII—USING PHONETIC RECOGNITION OF LETTERS

Phonetic identification of letters may occur naturally in some brain-damaged children after they have used sight-memory words for a time. This beginning awareness will be expressed by, "Why, 'dog' and 'dad' both start with the same sound." Or, " 'Betty' and 'Bill' both look the same at the beginning."

The verbal identification of letters should be done by two simultaneous identifications. Teach the *name* and the *sound* of a letter at the same time. Simultaneous identification is recommended because of the difficulty brain-damaged children experience in relating different phases of a learning procedure. Techniques to aid phonetic identification of letters include:

1. Use flash cards that present *both* the manuscript and cursive forms of the letter, both upper- and lower-case. In one unit of time, the child simultaneously associates four forms as representing one letter. He may not use all of these forms at this time, but once the association is made, he can be taught to use the appropriate form when necessary:

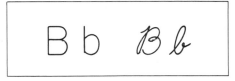

FIGURE 10-15

2. Teach the consonants first, beginning with those having sounds which are obviously different, such as "k," "p," "t." Teach the vowels next, with the long and the short sounds being learned simultaneously. The teacher should remind, "The long sound of the letter says its own name." A flash card for the simultaneous learning, involving visual and auditory, is illustrated, using the vowel, "a":

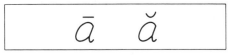

FIGURE 10-16

3. With some brain-damaged children, teaching is effective if flash cards are prepared for the vowels, always using the color red to represent the long sound, and the color green to represent the short sound. Follow through by writing new words with the same color cueing for the vowel sounds. Eventually, the colors can be eliminated.

4. Provide excellent reinforcement for learning the names and sounds of letters by projecting the letters, one by one, on a screen in front of the room. Use the color cueing mentioned in

the previous technique, if desired. Use an overhead projector, a 35 mm projector, or a film-strip projector. Instruct the children to tell about a particular letter when it appears. At first, allow the children plenty of time for thinking about the names and sounds of the letters. As learning proceeds, flash the letters on the screen at a more rapid pace, so that the verbal response to the visual stimulus must be more instantaneous. With this method, even hyperactive children know WHERE to look!

5. Phonetic reading can be taught to some brain-damaged children even though they cannot say the individual sounds because of limited speech ability. The following activities are a double-check to be sure the child knows the letter sounds:

   a. Say the sound of the letter and have the child point to the appropriate symbol. Start with a limited number of choices. The child may be able to use a typewriter for his answer.

   b. Have the children close their eyes and listen carefully. Tell them you are going to study a certain sound, as, for example, the "M" sound. Then say a number of words, some of which begin with "M." Have the child raise his hand when he hears the word beginning with the correct sound.

   c. Use workbooks for pre-reading. These will give a letter, and the child is to select the pictures of objects which begin with that sound. The child with learning problems should complete two or three workbooks of the same level, as recommended for the preprimer.

STEP IX—TYING TOGETHER PHONICS AND WORD-BUILDING

Now put phonetic sounds together. Start with two-letter words as well as combinations of letters which do not make up a word, but which the child should learn to pronounce, such as "ŏnt," or "bŏt." The student sounds out the combinations. At this step of learning, begin to teach the phonetic blend sounds.

It should be noted that a child who is handicapped in his *auditory discrimination* will have difficulty identifying *what* the sound is as well as *where* such a sound comes in a word. He will have difficulty identifying whether a sound is at the beginning or end of the word. He may say that the last sound of s-a-t is "s." Remedial activities should include those for auditory discrimination. (See Chap. 6.)

Some brain-damaged children cannot learn to put together sounds to make a word. Johnson and Myklebust distinguish between the visual and the auditory dyslexic, and recommend distinct teaching procedures.[2] When it is impossible for the child to put phonetic parts together to make a whole word, reverse the teaching procedure, and teach these children word development by starting with the *whole* word, and drawing the phonetic sounds *from the whole into the parts.*

STEP X–SPELLING

When the child has mastered the sounds of the letters, he can put them together to make simple words. The more meaningful the word is to the child, the more easily it will be learned. The child's sight-vocabulary will be a help at this step. He will rediscover words he already knows in terms of the letters which make them.

Spelling will be particularly difficult for a child who cannot sound out a word, or who cannot recall what a word looks like "in his mind." In the first case, the remedial procedures will include those necessary for *whole-to-part* learning. For example, present the word, written in anagrams, so that the child actually manipulates the word into its syllables or phonetic sounds. In the second case, acquiring internal visualization requires sight-memory, auditory-memory, and tactual-memory exercises.

Do not expect the child to be able to use even the words that he can read for writing compositions of his own, until you are sure he is able to revisualize and then integrate the words accurately in his mind.

---

[2]Doris J. Johnson and Helmer R. Myklebust, *Learning Disabilities* (New York and London: Grune and Stratton, 1967).

chapter 11

Pre-Writing

Writing demands many prerequisites. And a distinction must be made between the child's ability to simply *copy* forms—as letters—and his ability to *express* his ideas in writing. Both abilities require perceptual-motor coordination for producing the letters, but certainly the latter is a more involved and more advanced accomplishment. Written expression utilizes combinations of sensory input and output. The child must learn to express himself through symbols. Therefore, he must remember previous sensory input so that it can be correlated, sequenced, and then expressed by an exacting eye-hand skill.

READINESS

Readiness for pre-writing includes laterality, directionality, arm-hand coordination, eye-hand coordination, ocular control, the correction of perseveration, and the concept of terms such as:

right-left	one, two, three
up-down	around
top-bottom	across
in-out	middle, center
under-over	curve
beginning-end	trace
tall-short	vertical
on-off	horizontal
big-little	circle
oblique, diagonal, slanting	straight line

The pupil's dominant hand should be used most extensively. However, markings should be practiced with both hands, reinforcing pattern concept as well as the coordination of both sides of the body.

Pre-writing markings of major concern include, in order of increasing muscular control, variations of the *circle*, the *curved line*, and *vertical, horizontal, and oblique lines*. Three generalizations apply to the teaching of all of these markings:

1. Move from *freedom to confinement*. While initial markings are not confined, gradually require the child to *start* and *stop* within definite boundaries, using templates for children having particular difficulty. A set of templates proceeds from large to smaller areas of confinement:

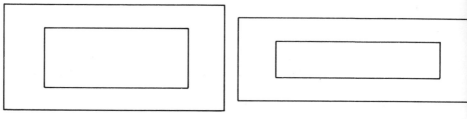

FIGURE 11-1

Next, confine by boxing in an area with horizontal and/or vertical lines. Emphasize confining lines by thickness, color, or textures such as gummed tape and crepe paper:

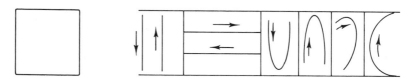

FIGURE 11-2

Use graph paper for guidelines for diagonals. Afterwards, the student may color his design:

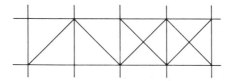

FIGURE 11-3

2. Progress from working at *large areas*, such as the chalkboard, to *smaller areas*, such as a piece of paper.

3. Make the majority of markings from *left to right*. This also compliments pre-reading readiness.

Techniques for teaching pre-writing overlap those already recommended in Chap. 10 for pre-reading.[1] The need for both gross-motor and fine-motor learning is emphasized again. Activities concerning the circle, square, and triangle should be adapted for teaching curved and straight lines. Using the techniques of Chap. 10 as a basis, further steps specifically for pre-writing markings include:

STEP I–THE CIRCLE

Motivate drawing by using interesting references and patterns. Refer to the circle as a baseball, beachball, hoop, soap bubble, cookie, or snowball, for example. Promote simple drawings:

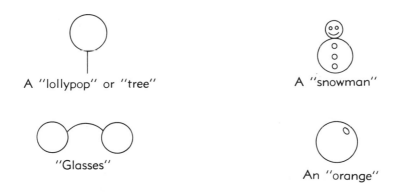

A "lollypop" or "tree"

A "snowman"

"Glasses"

An "orange"

FIGURE 11-4

STEP II–CURVES

Drawing a regulated curve (arc) demands more control than drawing a circle, probably because, in the former, perseveration interferes

---

[1]Also refer to *The Frostig Program for the Development of Visual Perception,* by Marianne Frostig and David Horne (Chicago: Follett Publishing Company, 1964).

with stopping, and also because directions must vary. Movements using the abductor muscles (*away* from the median axis of the body) are generally easier than those involving the adductor muscles (*toward* the median axis of the body.) Practice for abductor muscles includes:

FIGURE 11-5

Practice for adductor muscles involves the same curves drawn in the *opposite* direction. Provide templates for practicing arcs:

FIGURE 11-6

Markings using both abductor and adductor motions necessitate the student's learning to "change directions" as he works:

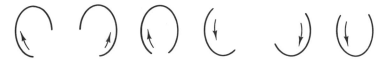

FIGURE 11-7

Include the drawing of arcs in activities that are fun:

1. Play "Jack, Jump Over the Candlestick" on the chalkboard. Draw a candle, with an X about one foot away on each side of it. The class can recite the nursery rhyme while one member draws an arc from the left-hand X to the right-hand X, going *over* the candle. Repeat, going *under* the candle.

2. Use the poem "Wee Willy Winky," going "upstairs" and "downstairs":

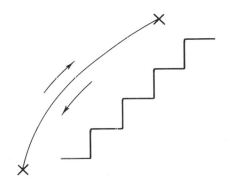

FIGURE 11-8

3. Use numerous figures involving arcs. (See Fig. 11-9, p. 150.)

STEP III—HORIZONTAL LINES

The straight, horizontal line is important, both for constructing letters, and for use as a guideline in space on which letters are to be written. The child will stay on this guideline better if he puts it there himself, or if it is emphasized in color. Use chalkboards that have permanently ruled (barely visible) horizontal lines on them, which the

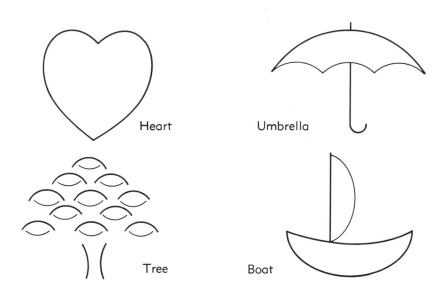

FIGURE 11-9. Develop forms from arcs. (Refer to p. 149.)

children can trace when they need a distinct guide. A ruler may be needed to help with the tracing. Be sure the child understands the term, "horizontal."

When exploring a straight line, take advantage of textures about the room. Have the child feel the rough cement lines between smooth ceramic tiles, the mortar lines between bricks, and the edges of doors, windows, and desks. Also have him feel the lines produced on pegboards or by folded paper. Other techniques are:

1. Elaborate on balance activities by having the child experience the rung of a ladder as a straight unit (line) in space. Prop up one end of the ladder about two feet high. The child should start at the low end and gradually approach rungs over which he must step very high, walking as he would in deep snow! (See the photograph at the beginning of this chapter.) Put the ladder on its side so the child can crawl in and out, around each rung. Then repeat the exercise, going backwards. Fasten a ladder against a wall. The child should climb it, stepping on the "straight lines" as he moves up and down.

2. Begin the child's marking of a freehand, horizontal line by having him connect two X's. Use color cueing by making the X

on the left in green, the other in red. Instruct, "*Start* at the left X, go to the right X, and *stop*." Also direct the child to go in the opposite direction. Finally request, "Go back and forth" (in a continuous activity between the X's). In this way, the child practices reversing his movements at the end of a line. Reinforce these techniques with a verbal "right," "left," "across," and "back."

STEP IV—VERTICAL LINES

Adapt techniques recommended for the horizontal line to the vertical line, reinforcing these with "up" and "down." Next, introduce the construction of a cross (plus sign) involving the bisection of a vertical and a horizontal line, and, finally, promote numerous designs which combine straight lines and circles. (See Fig. 11-10, p. 152.)

STEP V—OBLIQUE LINES

The construction of an oblique (diagonal, slanting) line is a very new process for the child, compared to his construction of the vertical and the horizontal lines. Much experimentation with the oblique lines is needed to reinforce its "sideways motion." Have the child practice the line in both the up and down directions. Finally, have him mark up and down in a continuous process, so that he reverses his movements at the end of a line. Next, introduce the "X," involving the bisection of an oblique line. Encourage designs that use diagonals. (See Fig. 11-11, p. 153.)

STEP VI—WORKING FOR A CONTINUITY OF MOTIONS INVOLVING CURVES AND STRAIGHT LINES

As the child practices marking curves and straight lines, it has been emphasized that he should experience these in all directions: up, down, right, left, and even "to and fro," which is a direction the child explores as he works at a table and moves his hand away from and toward his body. (The "to and fro" is a different directional experience from moving the hand up and down at the chalkboard.) It may be much more difficult for a child to trace a design in a right-to-left direction than in a left-to-right direction, but it is necessary that the variations

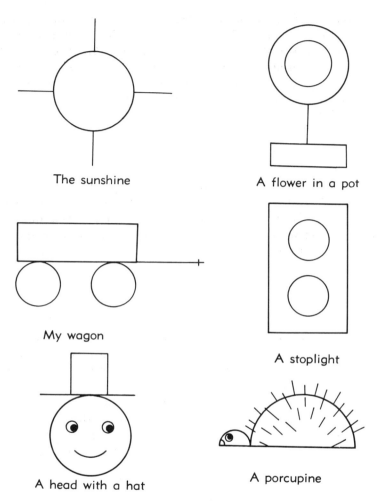

The sunshine

A flower in a pot

My wagon

A stoplight

A head with a hat

A porcupine

FIGURE 11-10. Designs combining straight lines and circles. (Refer to p. 151.)

be employed, both for the feedback of experiencing the spatial changes, and for the improvement of wrist and hand coordination.

When the child is relaxed in tracing a design in definite directions, develop designs which change direction *during a continuous process.* This helps to carry the child into a *progression* of movements developed from the isolated ones he has been learning. (See Figs. 11-12 and 11-13, pp. 154-155.)

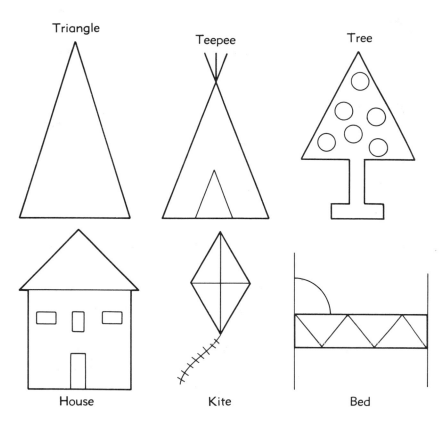

FIGURE 11-11. Designs that use diagonals. (Refer to p. 151.)

STEP VII—TRANSPOSING MARKINGS

Kephart describes the task set for the child when asked to copy or transpose.[1] This is an advanced step and may involve many different materials and combinations: chalkboard to chalkboard, chalkboard to pegboard, pegboard to pegboard, pegboard to paper, chalkboard to paper, paper to paper, paper to chalkboard, pegboard to chalkboard, and paper to pegboard. (See Fig. 11-14, p. 156.)

---

[1]Kephart, *The Slow Learner in the Classroom.*

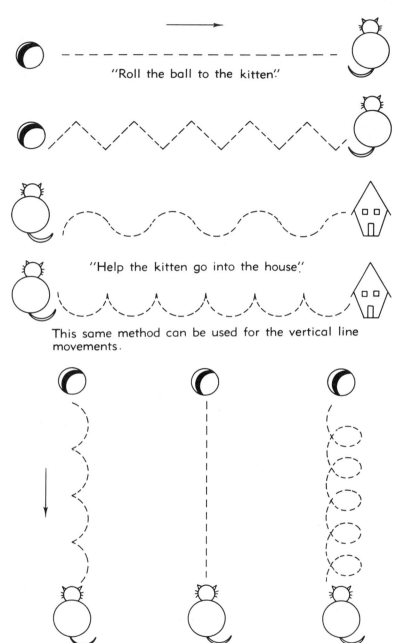

"Roll the ball to the kitten."

"Help the kitten go into the house."

This same method can be used for the vertical line movements.

FIGURE 11-12. Teach a progression of movements. (Refer to p. 152.)

"Lazy Eight"

FIGURE 11-13. Encourage continuous movements in all directions. (Refer to p. 152.)

STEP VIII—THE CONCEPT OF "BELOW," "ABOVE," AND "ON" A LINE

Be sure the child understands, "Make your markings *on the line.*" In Fig. 11-15, p. 156, the blocks are all "on the line."

Make a distinction between "on the line," "above the line," "against the line," "touching the line," and "along a line," so that the child knows *where* to write. Make the examples concrete by having the student arrange objects so they sit *on a line*, as letters do. (See Fig. 11-16, p. 157.)

FIGURE 11-14. Transposing is an advanced step. (Refer to p. 153.)

Introduce the concepts of "above a line" and "below a line," in preparation for letters such as y and j, which are written partly "below" the line. Finally, the child should be able to reproduce the markings he has learned, in relation to the horizontal line. (See Fig. 11-17, p. 157.)

STEP IX—DIFFERENTIATING SIZE

Teach the difference between "tall and short," "big and small," and "large and small," particularly for confined markings. A dotted line guides the top of the short markings. (See Fig. 11-18, p. 157.) It may be necessary to emphasize the spatial translation by colored guides such as dots or X's. (See Fig. 11-19, p. 158.)

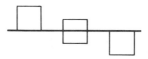

FIGURE 11-15. The blocks are all "on the line." (Refer to p. 155.)

FIGURE 11-16.   Put concrete objects on a line. (Refer to p. 155.)

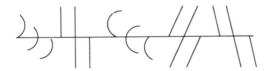

FIGURE 11-17.   Relate to a special guide—the horizontal line. (Refer to p. 156.)

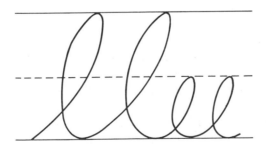

FIGURE 11-18.   Provide dotted line guides for short markings. (Refer to p. 156.)

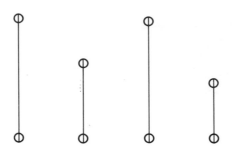

FIGURE 11-19. Emphasize spatial translation by distinct guides. (Refer to p. 156.)

Before the child begins STEP X, he should indicate his knowledge of letter size. For example, on the line below the letters, he can draw a short or tall vertical line:

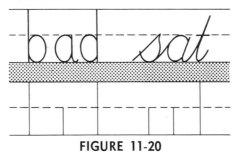

FIGURE 11-20

STEP X—BEGINNING THE WRITING OF LETTERS

There are no rigid rules regarding the teaching of either manuscript printing or cursive writing to the child with brain dysfunction. Normal children are expected to make a transition from manuscript printing to cursive writing, but this is very difficult and often impossible for the brain-damaged child who avoids adjustments. If the child's hand coordination is so poor that he can barely manage vertical and horizontal lines, then his written expression must be limited to manuscript forms. However, it is necessary to keep in mind that many such children are also visually limited, and may see an A or an E, for example, as pictured in Fig. 11-21, p. 159.

Where perceptual-motor coordination allows the formation of cursive letters, cursive writing (perhaps modified) should be the ultimate goal of written expression. Cursive writing emphasizes the relationship between letters, so that *whole words* are seen. Also, cursive writing is a more rhythmical procedure than manuscript printing, and the

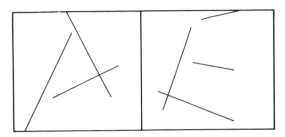

FIGURE 11-21. Letters may break apart for the visually impaired.
(Refer to p. 158.)

"rhythmical whole" of a word encourages the child to complete it, once it has been started. The child *feels* the motion of what he is producing, and is stimulated to finish the word in the same way he completes a rhythmical saying or a musical expression. Because cursive letters are connected with one another, a word written in cursive may be more easily structured by a child having difficulty with spacing and letter alignment.

Small, cursive letters begin at the line, and the child has a *starting point* in space which helps him to "get going." From this point, instruct him to move in specific directions, such as "up," or "to the right," in order to continue a letter. For a $\mathcal{t}$, instruct the child to start at the bottom, horizontal line and to make a tall, vertical line. Then he is to trace the same line back down, from top to bottom, finally crossing the figure with a short, horizontal line.

It may take the brain-damaged child longer to master some letters in cursive than in manuscript, not because of the form perception, but because of the more intricate hand movements involved in cursive writing. The cursive letters with loops, such as $\mathcal{l}$ and $\mathcal{e}$, are not as difficult as those letters requiring a reversal, tracing, or stopping of movement, such as $\mathcal{o}$, c, $\mathcal{b}$, $\mathcal{p}$, $\mathcal{g}$, $\mathcal{h}$ and $\mathcal{s}$. The capital letters of cursive are more intricate than capital manuscript letters. Therefore, if necessary, *modify* cursive writing by substituting capital letters of the upper case manuscript. Some of the most difficult capital, cursive letters are $\mathcal{F}$, $\mathcal{G}$, $\mathcal{H}$, $\mathcal{I}$, $\mathcal{J}$, $\mathcal{L}$, $\mathcal{S}$, $\mathcal{T}$, and $\mathcal{Y}$.

While the break between each manuscript letter within a word is detrimental to visual perception, and actually causes some children to forget what letter comes next, it may be helpful for other children who live only in "moments of time." Since it is difficult for these children to be sure about what comes next, the break before each letter gives time for thought.

TEACHING MANUSCRIPT PRINTING

Several general techniques for adapting manuscript printing for the brain-damaged are:

1. Teach the child to print letters with a *continuous stroke*, if possible, rather than with segmented lines. This holds the parts of the letter together, and helps the child to see the letter as a whole:

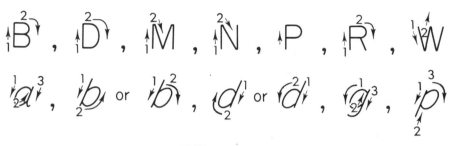

FIGURE 11-22

2. Try to give the child a *starting point in space*. There are children who cannot begin a capital L when it is written ⌐L , but who will do very well when the bottom line is used as their beginning guide so they can write ⌐L . Writing the capital L in this unusual manner violates the left-to-right, and top-to-bottom generalization, but it may be the only way a particular child can learn. Some other manuscript capital letters which can be started at the bottom, horizontal guideline (in addition to that given above) include:

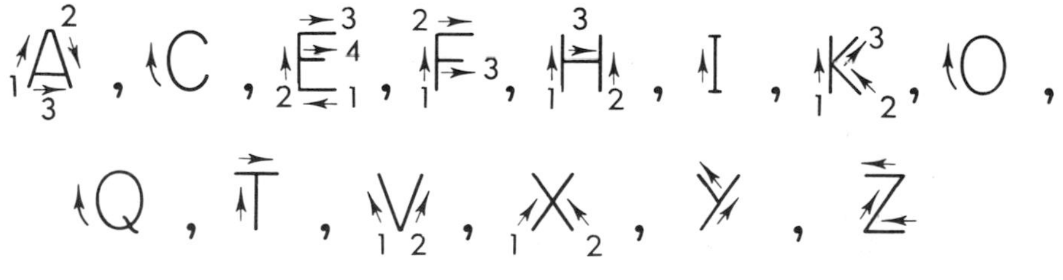

FIGURE 11-23

In summary, letters A, B, C, D, E, F, H, I, K, L, M, N, O, P, Q, R, S, T, V, X, Y, and Z can use the bottom line as a starting point. Therefore, for a child who is almost entirely limited to making movements *away* from himself (using abductor muscles), the *upper-case manuscript* may be his best solution for writing. Letters a, c, g, i, j, m, n, o, p, q, r, s, u, v, w, x, y, and z have a *starting* point at the *middle line*, halfway between the top and bottom lines. Letters c, e, i, u, s, x, and z can be started at the bottom line, if it is easier for the child. Letters b, d, f, h, k, l, and t *start* at the top line. Of these letters, f, k, l, and t can be started at the bottom line if necessary.

3. Apply *spatial directions* to letter construction, so that the pattern of the letter is securely related to the child's points of reference as established by his awareness of laterality and directionality. A manuscript *a* is: "Make a circle, and then trace down the right-hand side." The reference to spatial positions becomes particularly important when children are taught to write by way of earphones:

FIGURE 11-24

4. Experiment by associating a letter with something of interest to the child. Sometimes the association is distracting, but often

it helps recall. "A" is an Indian tepee, with a line across it; "Q" is a circle with a tail on it; "E" is a straight, vertical line with three legs on it; "S" looks like a worm; "T" looks like a telephone pole.

STEP XI—INTERNAL VISUALIZATION OF FORMS

The ten steps for pre-writing, already given, particularly apply to the child's ability to copy some form of written expression. Use of these steps will also assist the child's internal visualization of letters and words. This visualization can be reinforced and further developed by image-memory exercises, until the child can visualize and then reproduce letters (and eventually words) by way of auditory (dictating) and tactual (tracing with the fingers, and skin-writing) cueing, as well as the visual. Refer to Chap. 7 dealing with conceptualization, for techniques to strengthen the *organization* of ideas to be expressed in writing.

chapter 12

Pre-Arithmetic
Counting and Number Concepts

Pre-arithmetic readiness includes memory and sequencing activities, and form perception. (See Chap. 10.) The child can then identify forms to be "counted," and, eventually, the numerals themselves.

STEP I—VERBALIZING NUMBERS

Rhymes such as "One, Two, Buckle My Shoe" or "Ten Little Indians" are hummed or sung by children before they have the concept of the words. This verbalization helps the child to memorize the names of the numbers, particularly those from one to ten. Reinforce the rote memory in the classroom:

1. Include *songs*, *finger exercises*, and *rhymes* with rhythmical number verbalizations.

2. *Repeat numbers* during opening exercises for the day, to reinforce an auditory or visual pattern. Teach that *zero* comes before one, and means "nothing," or "none," or "not any there." Otherwise, at a later time, "zero" baffles the slow learner, as he trys to comprehend such mathematical operations as subtracting zero from two.

STEP II—REALIZING THAT UNITS (NUMBERS) EXIST

The child needs to experiment with the meaning of a "unit" until the oneness or distinctness of this unit is realized and expressed easily.

The importance of this step is the *recognition of a UNIT in time* and space. Work toward this definition by involving gross-motor, fine-motor, tactual, auditory, and visual techniques:

1. Coordinate the verbalization of a unit with *jumping* up and down on the *trampoline*. At first, as the child jumps, the teacher speaks. Later, the child carefully coordinates each jump with each verbal expression of his own. Even a child with braces can be placed on a trampoline with an adult jumping carefully beside him to let him feel the meaning of a unit. At this step, verbalization reinforces the experience, but the numbers do not have to be in sequential order. Repeating only *one word*, such as, "One, one, one" is satisfactory. Vary the technique by having the child say the word he likes, or a word on which he is working for speech therapy.

2. Have the child do *physical exercises* such as push-ups, going up and down stairs, chin-ups on a chinning bar, and jumping rope. Add verbalization.

3. Convert *songs and rhymes* to experiences. At the end of a poem such as "Jack Be Nimble," the child can jump back and forth over a pretend candle, speaking each time he jumps.

4. Surprise the student by providing crutches (appliances for body support) that he must learn to use. Require one step with the crutches each time the child says a word. This technique forces a motor activity on which the child works hard as he coordinates movements with each unit of verbalization.

5. Put large, flat rocks into each of the child's hands, and have him beat these together each time he speaks. The vibration of the rock over the palm of the hand provides excellent feedback, and the sharp sounds of the rocks give auditory reinforcement.

STEP III—COUNTING AS AN ORDERLY RHYTHMICAL PROCESS

Most brain-damaged children break down in the *rhythmic progression* necessary for naming one number after another. The progression of units is not smooth and orderly. Therefore, in addition to experiencing a unit, it is necessary for the child to learn to express units in a systematic, continuous pattern. If the definite, regular beat is not realized by the child, even his verbal counting will be irregular, as diagrammed:

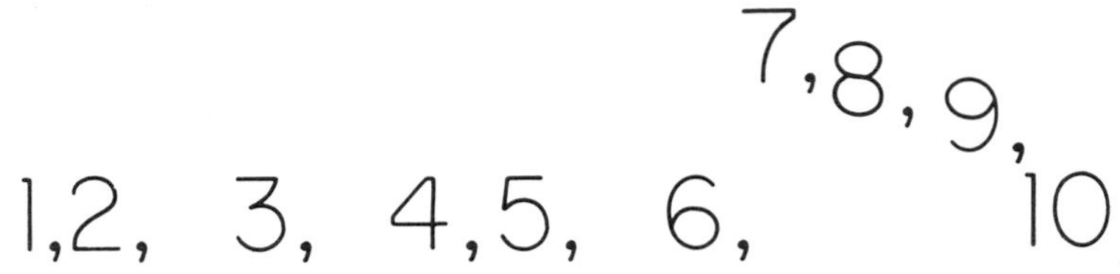

$$7,8,9,$$
$$1,2, \quad 3, \quad 4,5, \quad 6, \qquad 10$$

FIGURE 12-1

For this step, the exercises outlined in STEP II should be practiced until there is an orderly progression of expression. (Refer to the discussion of synchrony and rhythm in Chap. 5.) Rhythmic activities of all kinds reinforce this step, and are a readiness prerequisite for arithmetic.

1. "Count" *objects into containers*. Start with cubical counting blocks, all of the same color.
   a. Ask the student to put *one* (or *a*, or *the*) block into a container. Vary the type of container (carton, teacher's hand, can, basket, box, bowl, glass, pail, etc.) to encourage motivation. The child should grasp the cube, lift it over the container, and drop it. In this way, *seeing* and touching are employed, with an *auditory* reminder when the cube hits the hard container. Reinforce by a single verbal command, such as "One," or "Now." (It should be noted that while sound is an excellent reinforcement for some children, it is distracting to others.) If a child moves a block too fast to correlate it with his verbal expression, regulate the pace by having him relax momentarily between each count: "Block" (hands to his side), "Block" (hands to his side), etc. If necessary, regulate pacing more rigidly by *handing* the child a block each time it is to be counted.
   b. When the child performs well with like blocks, vary the color or form of the objects, to increase concentration. Then the verbalization may be, "Red block, blue block, yellow tee," for example. A child may be motivated by: "collecting" stones to bring to class for counting; playing store with coins; counting poker chips, beans, the half-shells of English

walnuts, petals of a flower, colored eggs in a bird's nest, toy soldiers standing in a row, tiny objects inside a colored box, and pretend cookies (cardboard) into a cookie jar.

2. Use a form board to structure "counting," as recommended in the Appendix.

3. Have the child "count" cubes into *Stern trays*.[1] A separate tray is required for each number being learned.

FIGURE 12-2

4. Have the child listen to *piano keys*, "counting" the number of black or white keys. He hears, sees, and feels each key he counts. Use the keys of a xylophone.

5. Begin to teach the child with an *abacus*, which is later used for arithmetic problems. Start with only one row of big beads. Use an abacus with removable rods so that the color of the beads can be changed, and also more rows can be added.

6. Devise techniques to make counting more automatic by requesting the child to "count" objects while he particularly notes *where* to place them:

    a. "Count" *blocks* onto plain sheets of paper of varying colors.

    b. Place "counted" blocks *inside* or *around* a large circle, square, triangle, or lines drawn on a piece of paper.

    c. "Count" and arrange blocks around the edge of a paper,

---

[1]Catherine Stern, *Structural Arithmetic Series* (Boston: Houghton Mifflin Company).

or *above, below,* or *on* a heavy line drawn on paper. Use vertical, horizontal, and oblique lines, reinforcing the child's concepts of "above," "below," "along," "straight," and "oblique."

d. Use a *Montessori Board* (a gradation of cylinders) as a "counting" device.

e. Have the child "count" *pegs* as they are put into and taken out of pegboard. Golf tees may be counted as they are put into acoustical tile, or into perforated masonite mounted on styrofoam. Plastic spoons may be counted as they are stuck into and taken out of slits in the side of a box, and rings as they are put on and taken off a peg.

STEP IV—ORGANIZING OBJECTS TO BE RECOGNIZED (COUNTED)

In this step, stop and teach the child how to organize his work. *Total* organization cannot be taught at this point, but the child needs some idea of what "organization" means before he can approach learning intelligently and efficiently. Organization prior to counting cannot be stressed too much, since the disorganization of a brain-damaged child is extremely detrimental to his work with numbers. Most brain-damaged children look at a group of objects, and attempt to count them in the same disorderly grouping they see. The result is disorderly counting—some objects are counted two or three times, and some are never counted at all. Two methods of organizing objects are presented here, in order of increasing difficulty:

1. Have the child *pick up an object in a group and methodically move it* from one place to another, treating each object as a separate unit which can be *seen* and *manipulated*. Begin with only a few objects. Verbalize each time the object is moved, such as "Block, block, block, block." This type of "counting" is a basic method, but it is limited in that all things to be counted cannot always be moved.

2. Teach the child to organize by *rearranging objects* so that they can be identified from *left to right*, or from *top to bottom*. Now the child can "count" the objects by *looking*, and by *touching*. Rearranging into organized groupings requires that the child have a sense of spatial relationships; otherwise, going "from left

to right" or "from top to bottom" will have no meaning, and the new arrangement will be just as difficult to count as the first grouping.

While rearranging, at first make rows very straight, to avoid confusion. Then, as learning occurs, in order to prepare the child for counting objects which cannot be manipulated (as those on paper), put some objects a little out of line so that the child must decide how to count them while considering the whole grouping:

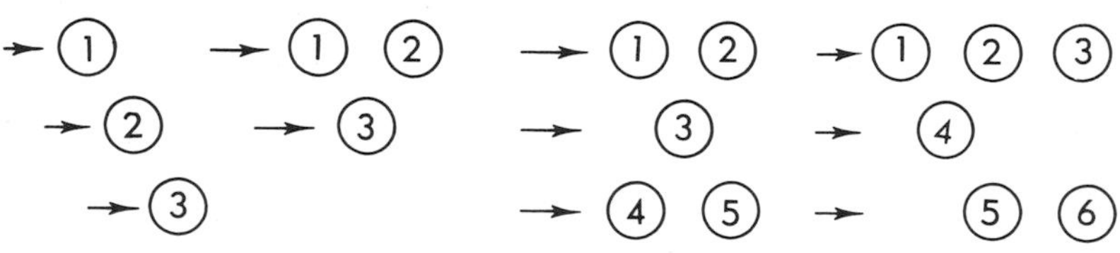

FIGURE 12-3. Counting irregular patterns.

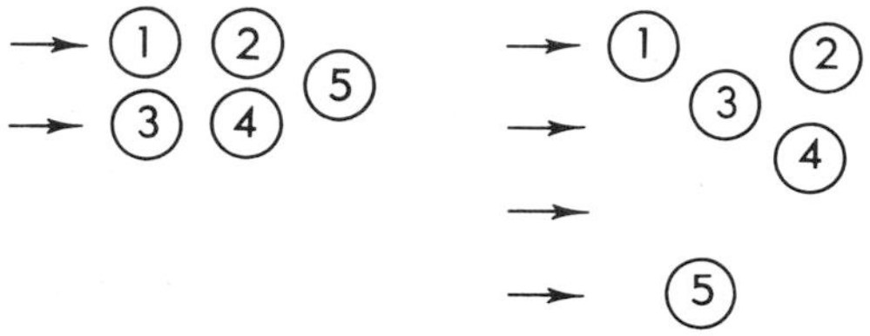

FIGURE 12-4. Counting very irregular patterns.

STEP V—VERBALIZING THE SEQUENTIAL ORDER OF NUMBERS

When the child has learned to "count" objects systematically, begin to teach that the sequential order of units are identified by specific names (numbers). Repeat all of the exercises recommended in STEP III, but give the correct number to each object, "One, two, three, four, five, six, etc."

In (1) under STEP III, if the child is asked to count *two* blocks into a container, at first make only two blocks available. As learning proceeds, provide more blocks, instructing, "Count out two blocks." It may be necessary to use some physical means to *stop* the activity at two, since most children continue counting until all the blocks are used. If a child has trouble stopping, instruct him to do some action which absolutely breaks the continuity of his counting, such as, "Count three blocks into this dish, and when you are done, put your hands on the table." Additional exercises include:

1. String *beads* for the child to count. Start with large beads of the same color.

2. Have the child paste and count *squares of colored paper* along vertical, horizontal, or oblique lines. The child then has a project he can take home to keep his parents informed of his progress.

3. Instruct the child to build a *tall tower* and to count the number of blocks in it.

4. Place *beanbags* (flat, and 7 inches in diameter) on a child's head while he counts. Have him walk around the room balancing the beanbags he has counted. There is always a race to see who can balance the most beanbags.

5. As the child lies on a *long, wooden bench*, instruct him to slap the side of it a certain number of times, with either or both hands. (This is also a good exercise for reinforcing laterality.)

6. *Verbally* request the child to draw a certain number of objects. This step is harder than the previous ones, as the child is requested to create the objects himself.

STEP VI—INTRODUCING WRITTEN SYMBOLS FOR NUMBERS

A child is exposed regularly to the written symbol for a number. Therefore, even before this step, it is probable that he is associating a symbol with the units he has been experiencing. The verbal counting of numbers is intentionally presented *before* the child's introduction to the written symbol, since the latter is learned more easily when the child has some awareness of its meaning. Methods for introducing the visual symbol for verbal and visual identification include:

1. Match symbols with *three-inch square number cards* the children can use at their desks. Provide several cards of each number being learned. Any deck of cards with numbers on them can also be used. Learning is fun for the children when it is a

game, and the one who matches or "slaps" the most card pairs, wins. Later, use the number cards for *flash cards*.

2. Put *number cards* around the room so that they can be seen when a number is spoken. Use *flannelboard numbers*, naming them as they are put on and taken off the board.

3. Use the child's own *street address* and *telephone number* to stimulate interest. Provide a dial telephone in the classroom; also encourage parents to help their child with phone calls at home.

4. Play *bingo* for fun. Give each child a card with varying number combinations from 1 through 10. Name a number which the child, in turn, covers with a piece of cardboard. Vary this method by writing the number on the chalkboard instead of naming it verbally.

5. Provide *dice* made from small cardboard boxes or wooden blocks. Paint numbers on the sides so that the child can identify the number he rolls.

6. Make a *number-tree*, with each child contributing a numbered leaf. Or, let it "rain" numbers. (See Fig. 12-5, p. 173.)

7. Project *transparent slides* of individual numbers, verbally identifying each for reinforcement.

8. Look for numbers everywhere: on pictures, street signs, calendars, clocks, etc. Encourage the child to tell about numbers he sees at home. Provide old calendars with big squares so that the child can copy the number in each square.

9. Play *"Password"* with numbers, as recommended in Chap. 10.

LEARNING NUMBERS ABOVE NINE

Align the teens vertically, so that the child can *see* that they all begin with a 1. Point out that 10, 11, and 12 begin with 1 even though they do not say "teen." Have the child underline or circle the first number in each series, as the teens, twenties, etc. Point out the first number "clue" to the series. Use color cueing to designate like numbers. If the number consists of two or more symbols, concepts of "left," "beginning," "start," "first," "last," "right," and "middle" become important. Numbers such as 13 and 31 will be reversed and identified as the same if the child has no concept of left and right. Poor awareness of spatial relationships hinders the child's learning that one number is placed "after" or "before" another.

FIGURE 12-5. Stimulate learning and motivation by use of number symbols. (Refer to p. 172.)

As learning proceeds, verbally describe a number as, "I see a number with a two in front and a four at the end. What is the number?" Often a child recalls only the last number he hears, and his reply is "4" or

"42." He has difficulty keeping the auditory sequence in mind. Then, teaching should include exercises in *auditory memory*. Such exercises applied to number recall and expression are a first step for handling numbers in an abstract manner.

STEP VII–PUTTING WRITTEN NUMBERS
IN SEQUENTIAL ORDER

As the child recognizes the numbers he sees, begin to teach the sequential order of the written symbols:

1. Show the child how to arrange *individual number cards* in correct order at his desk. Or, pass out one or more number cards to each student, and request him to put these in order along the front of the room. The students have to think hard about, "Who's number comes next?" Sequence numbers on the flannelboard, or paste paper symbols in correct order on a piece of paper. Ask the child to work independently, arranging numbers according to the *page numbers* in books. Look at a clock, writing the numbers in order.

2. Challenge a child to think about what comes next by having him fill in *missing numbers* of a sequence. The reply can be verbal or written. Start with a very simple sequence such as 0, ____, 2.

3. Prepare *dot-to-dot* exercises, being sure the numbers are large and clear enough for a brain-damaged child with a visual handicap.

4. Fold an 8-by-10 inch piece of light cardboard lengthwise so that there are 3-inch strips, each 8 inches long. Make nine slits along the edge of an outside fold, going from the long edge to a fold. Write the number symbols from 1 through 10, one on each flap. (See Fig. 12-2, p. 168.) When teaching, tuck occasional numbers inside the other, uncut, strip. The child is to name the symbol that is out of sight.

5. Prepare *color-by-number* exercises.

6. Weave a 10-by-12 inch *heavy paper mat*. Draw a clear, heavily outlined design on it. Then number, in order, each vertical strip of the design. Take the mat apart and show the child how to put it together again by putting the strips in the correct order:

FIGURE 12-6

7. Cut up two *calendars* with big numbers on them. Mount the pieces of one calendar, in order, on a contrasting, colored paper. Instruct the child to:

    a. Put the unmounted numbers on top of the matching, mounted number.

    b. Name the number on each square.

    c. Arrange the unmounted pieces in the same order as those mounted.

    d. Write the numbers in the same order as those that are mounted.

STEP VIII—ASSOCIATING WRITTEN NUMBER SYMBOLS WITH NUMBER CONCEPTS

1. Have the child count objects onto numbered squares or papers:

FIGURE 12-7

2. Use a *Counting Board*, such as the one pictured at the beginning of this chapter. Depending upon which number is placed in the rectangle at the left, instruct the child to place the same number of pegs in the holes at the right. The pegs are made of doweling, and the numbers are luminescent house numbers which the child can feel.

3. Make a hop-scotch pattern on the ground, writing a number in each square. After the child moves onto a square, he says the name of the number and claps or stomps that many times.

4. Have the child trace around his hand and then number each of the five or ten fingers.

5. If a child is particularly restless, put a series of numbers around a table, requesting the child to count out the appropriate number of colored sticks for each number as he moves around. (See Fig. 12-8, p. 177.)

6. Put numbers along a side of a sheet of paper. After, or below, each number the child should:
   a. draw the correct number of objects;
   b. paste the correct number of stickers;
   c. line up the correct number of sticks.

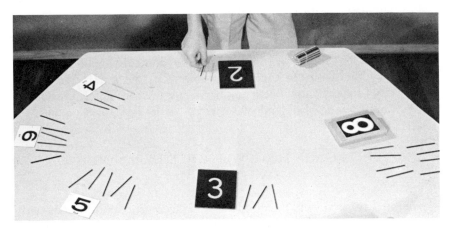

FIGURE 12-8. Use concrete techniques for matching number symbols and objects. (Refer to p. 176.)

Numerous printed exercises are commercially available for these types of lessons. The child must concentrate on making a form *while* he is counting. The more complicated the design, the more automatic his number concept must be.

STEP IX—COUNTING WITH DECREASING RELIANCE ON TACTILE CLUES

Not all objects can be concretely manipulated, as, for example, objects in a picture. But they still must be counted. There must be a transfer of the *tactile-visual* or *tactile-auditory* experiences of previous methods to a totally visual or auditory perception. This *transfer* is a transitional step toward abstract thinking which is necessary in learning arithmetic.

1. Prepare lessons for counting *objects pictured on paper*. If necessary, cut up the paper at first, to show the child each separate object. Gradually, instruct the child to count by *looking* at the paper and by *touching* it. The objects should first be presented in organized arrangements, then in arrangements of increased complexity as the child learns. Select uncluttered pictures which show definite objects. Many pictures can be cut from catalogues, magazines, and postcards. Vary the child's touching each object by having him circle, underline, or "X" it as he counts.

2. Have the child touch and count the dots in each configuration of *giant dominoes*. Be sure the child learns to count these while he points to the dots himself, *and* while the teacher points to the dots. Match like formations of the dominoes, and eventually play the game. In the giant domino set, the colors remain the same for each particular number configuration. Later, the smaller dominoes, in black and white, are a harder task for the child.

STEP X—COUNTING WITHOUT DEPENDING ON TACTILE CLUES

In this advanced step, the child is asked to count configurations without touching them. He must look at the form and then give the correct answer. Initially, he may have to count out loud. Many of the previously mentioned techniques can be repeated, omitting the tactile clues: flash cards, pictures from magazines, and dominoes. Other techniques are:

1. Prepare *card sets with varying patterns* of the same number to be sorted:

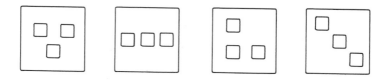

FIGURE 12-9

At first, use the same color for the patterns; later, provide varying colors:

FIGURE 12-10

This technique can be varied by using *different* shapes for the forms to be counted. Later, use these same cards to decide whether a number is larger or smaller than another.

2. Prepare card sets with numbers written on some cards, and with patterns of those numbers on others:

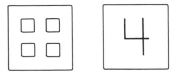

FIGURE 12-11

Repeat this technique for lotto games:

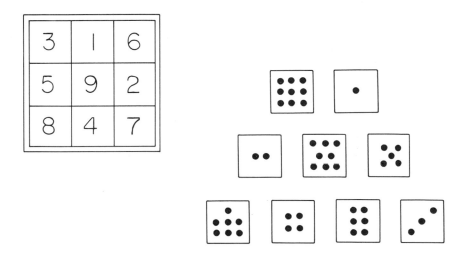

FIGURE 12-12. Board and cards for lotto game.

3. Count all types of visual configurations: the stripes on a piece of fabric, or on a flag; and cookies drawn on the chalkboard.

4. Have the child listen to all types of auditory stimuli, counting each unit. Gradually, increase the speed of the units as the child learns.

STEP XI—COMPARING UNITS

Help the child to discern the similarities and differences of the units with which he has been working. By comparing terms such as "the same as," "alike," "less than," and "more than," the relationship of the units, and groups of units, becomes more meaningful. Use the same teaching ideas expressed in previous steps of this chapter, but now *repeat* or duplicate the clues, so that the child can decide whether the second experience is the same as the first. An example of an auditory comparison would be to play *one* note on the piano; then instruct the child to listen carefully while one, or more, notes are played. Begin to teach, "Are they the same?"

STEP XII—BEGINNING ARITHMETIC

1. Try a game which can be played with one child, or several, in a classroom, in which the child must *think* of the answer to, "What number comes *after* 6?" etc. A little more difficult to answer is, "What number comes *before* 6?" Leading into arithmetic, ask, "What is 6 and 1 more?"

2. Use *arithmetic readiness books* to present lessons where concrete methods enable a child to compare numbers. Such a method is to *string beads* in alternating color and number patterns. In order to alternate the patterns the child must think, "How many more beads must I add to get the number I want?" Reinforce this technique, using the form board, or the peg board, and the abacus.

STEP XIII—LEARNING THE ORDINALS

The ordinal system is a more involved concept of numbers. It is not necessary for the child to know this concept before he begins his study of arithmetic.

1. After the child knows the correct order of the numbers, make a line of blocks, requesting, "Give me block number 3," etc.

2. Next, teach the child that "first" means the same as "1."

3. Finally, apply the ordinals to objects: "This is the first card on the flannelboard, and here is the second." Ask the child to select the first, second, or third object from a row of objects.

appendix

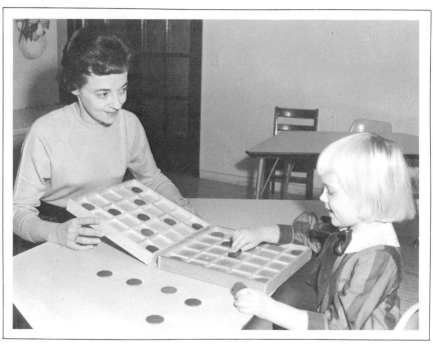

Appendix

Details for using the form board, and similar boards, for making patterns from parts, and for analyzing patterns, are described in this Appendix. These techniques can be adapted for many applications.

Provide a form board divided into two-inch squares. The sides of the squares should be raised so that they are one-quarter inch high. This sectioned form board makes it possible for the child to accomplish lessons, even with uncoordinated hand movements. Blocks, poker chips, and small pieces of paper will not move around because of the raised edges of the sections.

Use the sectioned form board to structure both *space and time*. The sections delineate specific areas to be used, and clearly define how one area is related to the next (top, bottom, left, or right). Timewise, an impulsive "crash-attack" on a form board lesson is not possible since one object is methodically placed *before* or *after* another.

TEACHING COLORS WITH THE FORM BOARD

STEP I—MATCHING COLORS

When first learning there are "colors," the child sorts one from another. At this point, it is not necessary that he know their names.

1. Have the child compare a color to WHITE. Have him sort RED and WHITE discs into separate piles, observing there is a difference in their COLOR. If he has difficulty comparing RED to WHITE, compare RED to BLACK. When the child knows the difference between RED and WHITE, or RED and BLACK, add a third color. The three to sort may be RED, BLACK, and WHITE, or, perhaps, WHITE, RED, and BLUE. Continue to add one different color as learning occurs.

2. As the child compares two, three, or more colors, make a design of these on the form board, requiring him to place chips or discs *exactly on top* of the design, matching like colors. Vary this technique by making the design with a one-inch cube in each section, requesting the child to place a like-colored cube beside the one already there.

3. After like objects of the same color are matched, *vary the type of objects*, but expect the child to still match the color. For example, place a piece of colored paper (or a miniature object) in each section of the form board, and request the child to put a matching chip or cube in each section.

4. Put blocks, chips, or colored paper in each section of the top, horizontal line of the form board, and require the child to align, *vertically*, *"under"* each, objects of the *same* color. Also use a similar exercise by aligning the colored objects along the left-hand, vertical side of the form board and then requiring the child to continue the matching, *horizontally*, *"after"* each colored object.

STEP II—VERBAL IDENTIFICATION

At this point, the child has matched colors through *visual* cueing. Now he should learn that colors have *verbal* names.

1. Direct, "Make a row of red (or another color) chips, like this first chip." Here, the teacher combines visual and verbal cues by *showing* and *naming* the correct chip.

2. After the student has correctly arranged the chips on the form board, ask him for a particular color. Direct, "Hand me a red chip," or "Hand me a blue block." Speed up the requests as the child learns, requiring him to think faster.

The child may enjoy being the teacher for a change, so let him give the same directions to you. Try to fool him occasionally by handing him the wrong-colored block. If he fails to notice that you are giving him the wrong block, recheck your evaluation of his knowledge of colors.

3. Ask the student to find objects of a specific color in the environment.

STEP III—READING THE NAMES OF THE COLORS

1. Across the top, or down the left-hand side of the form board, put a piece of paper in each section, with the *name of a color* printed on it. Have the student identify the name and color by putting the correctly colored object "*beneath*," "*beside*," or "*on*" the word that identifies it.

2. Refer to (2) in STEP VI of the pre-reading chapter for reinforcing the written identification of colors.

STEP IV—APPROACHING MEMORY THROUGH COLORS

The child should now name objects that he recalls to be always, or usually, a specific color:

An apple is usually red.
Sometimes, an apple is yellow.
The sky is blue.
My dad's car is brown.

If the child has trouble remembering, stimulate his thinking by asking:

"What color is a banana?"
"What color is your house?"

TEACHING PATTERN ANALYSIS AND DEVELOPMENT WITH THE FORM BOARD

When using the form board for pattern development, there are four important considerations:

1. *When a child studies a form or design, he should orient it in relation to himself,* and then orient the components in relation to one another. If he cannot do this automatically, he should be taught to do so. Otherwise, the design is perceived in a non-meaningful, disorganized fashion, without specific, stable points of reference. Teach the child to analyze a design by aligning its vertical center with his own vertical axis. A knowledge of laterality and directionality precedes his ability to begin this analysis. There will be parts of the design to the *right* or to the *left* of the child's vertical reference. There also will be components at the *top* and at the *bottom* of the design.

   To help a child analyze a design on the form board, it may be necessary, at first, to accentuate the *center axis* (or area) with a colored ribbon or marking.

2. *When transposing designs, consider where they are placed in relationship to one another.* The design from which the child is copying can be placed to the left, right, top, or bottom of the design the child is making. The different positions can affect the child's ability to copy the design, and the effect varies with the child. For instance, the child may be able to reproduce the design easily when it is to the *left* of his own form board, but he may experience great difficulty when the design to be copied is to the right, or to the top, or the bottom of his own form board. This discrepancy in ability to copy in all positions may be related to the child's ocular movements. Or, it may be related to an inflexibility in orienting the design in relation to himself.

3. *Make patterns more complicated by increasing the number of components, and/or the number of colors.*

4. *Proceed with definite purposes,* moving from *simple* designs involving one and then more components, to more complex designs. Proceed from *vertical* to *horizontal* to *diagonal* patterns.

STEP I—TRANSPOSING FROM ONE FORM BOARD TO ANOTHER

1. Place two form boards side by side. One is used by the teacher, the other by the student. Begin with designs involving one component. Put a block, or poker chip, in one of the four sections at the corners of the teacher's board, and ask the student to do the same with his. After he realizes where *one* item is to be placed at one corner, require the student to place an object in two, three, or four corners.

2. Next, develop patterns confined to a small board or to small areas of a larger board, which are easier for the child to copy than designs requiring scrutiny of the *whole* board. Do this by covering three-quarters or one-half of the board with a large piece of cardboard.

3. Since the *edge* of the form board acts as a stable guideline, produce initial patterns with the whole board which involve the corners of the board, or short, straight-line patterns along the sections of the outside rows:

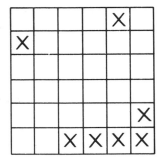   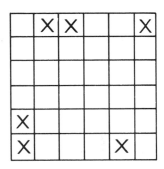

FIGURE A-1

4. Proceed now with vertical-line patterns. Those that are not along the outside of the board will be more difficult for the student, since a greater awareness of spatial relationships is required. After he has made the line, the child can *feel* what "vertical" means.

5. Introduce the horizontal line, finally combining it with the vertical:

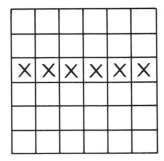   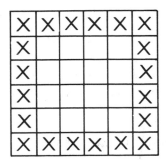   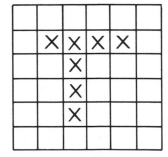

FIGURE A-2. Note that the third diagram requires more spatial awareness than the second.

6. Introduce the oblique line, and eventually develop patterns involving a combination of the horizontal, vertical, and oblique:

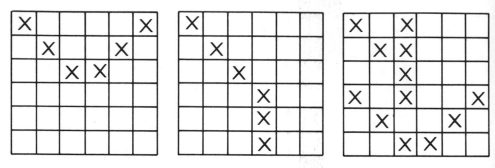

FIGURE A-3

7. With colored cubes or chips, develop *solid* designs on the form board. Start with only two colors, adding another only as learning progresses. By this method, in addition to the reinforcement of patterns, there can be a reinforcement of "vertical," "horizontal," "alternating," "sequencing," and "sorting":

R	B	R	B	R	B
R	B	R	B	R	B
R	B	R	B	R	B
R	B	R	B	R	B
R	B	R	B	R	B
R	B	R	B	R	B

FIGURE A-4. Horizontal alternating with vertical sorting.

8. Use a combination of blocks and chips for more intricate sequencing patterns. (See Fig. A-5, p. 189.)

STEP II—TRANSPOSING FROM PAPER TO THE FORM BOARD

Provide an advanced learning situation by having the child reproduce designs on the form board, copying from pieces of paper having

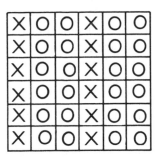

FIGURE A-5. X = a block, O = a chip. Develop patterns to teach sequencing. (Refer to p. 188.)

the same sections and size as the form board. In this way, the child can copy without requiring the constant one-to-one relationship with the teacher, who needs only to approve the finished design.

STEP III—TRANSPOSING SMALL PATTERNS TO LARGE ONES

Proceed to copying from paper designs smaller (as small as six-inches square) than the form board.

STEP IV—USING FOUR BLOCKS FOR EACH SECTION

Place as many as four blocks in each section, to make a more complicated design.

STEP V—TRANSPOSING FROM THE FORM BOARD TO PLAIN PAPER

Teach the child how to reproduce a form board design by placing blocks on plain paper. He will have no sections, as guides, to delineate the spaces. His ability to do this will affirm a beginning ability to structure tasks for himself.

TEACHING PRE-ARITHMETIC

STEP I—SYSTEMATICALLY IDENTIFYING A UNIT

Have the child put one block or chip into each section of the form board, moving from left to right or from top to bottom. Verbalize with one word to indicate each block, or unit, put into place, such as "One, one, one." Later, as two units are put into each section, verbally reinforce by, "One, two; one, two;" etc.

STEP II—COUNTING BY VERBAL IDENTIFICATION

Proceed along the sections of the form board as the student learns to count, verbally identifying each object with the correct *sequential number*. Systematically place one chip into each square, counting, "One, two, three, four," and so on. It is important that the chips are placed in the "next" available space on the form board, going either from left to right or from top to bottom. This method structures spacing and timing, and creates a pattern the child can see and feel.

STEP III—MATCHING NUMBER SYMBOLS

Put papers with numbers written on them in the sections of the form board. Give the child small papers with the same numbers on them, requesting him to place like numbers on top of those on the form board.

STEP IV—LEARNING NUMBER CONCEPTS

Put number symbols in the top row of sections, and direct the child to count out the correct number of blocks or chips in the sections below the numbers. A variety of number combinations are possible, depending upon whether chips or blocks are used, or a combination of both. Each section will hold four one-inch blocks, and more than one chip.

STEP V—COUNTING RANDOM DESIGNS

Many brain-damaged children are disorganized when counting objects scattered in front of them. The form board helps to organize counting by providing defined spaces going from left to right, and from top to bottom. For example, the eighteen components of the following pattern are counted:

1		2	3		4
		5	6		
7		8	9		10
		11	12		
13		14	15		16
		17	18		

FIGURE A-6

Finally, proceed to counting more random patterns:

	1		2		
		3		4	5
6			7		8
	9				
		10		11	12
13		14			15

FIGURE A-7

Index